THE LONE WOLF GAME DEVELOPERS TOOLKIT

Contents

Chapter 1:
Introduction to Solo Game
Development

Making a video game all by yourself is no small task. It requires a bunch of different skills, like programming, game design, art, and audio. It also requires a ton of organization, time management, and determination. But if you're up for the challenge, the rewards can be huge. As a solo game developer, you have complete control over your project and the freedom to work at your own pace. You also have the chance to learn new skills and get valuable experience that can help you move forward in your career.

Now, let's talk about the skills you'll need to make a game by yourself. Depending on the type of game you're making, you might need to know how to code in one or more programming languages. You'll also need to have a good understanding of game design principles and mechanics, so you can create a fun and engaging game. Art skills, like drawing and 3D modelling, are also important for creating the visuals and assets for your game. And if you're making a game with sound effects or music, you'll need some audio skills as well.

In addition to these technical skills, you'll also need to be super organized and good at managing your time. Making a game can take a long time, especially if you're doing it all by yourself, so it's important to set goals and priorities and stick to a schedule. This will help you stay on track and make progress. You'll also need to be able to manage your resources, whether that means budgeting your time and money or keeping track of all the assets and tools you'll need to build your game.

So, why would someone choose to make a game all by themselves? For one, you have complete creative control over your project. You get to make all the decisions and shape the game exactly how you want it. You also have the freedom to work at your own pace and set your own schedule. And if you're just starting out in game development, making a game by yourself can be a great way to learn new skills and gain valuable experience. It can also be a great way to get your foot in the door and start building a portfolio of work that you can show to potential employers or collaborators.

Creating a game completely solo is no easy feat. It requires a wide range of skills and a high level of organization, time management, and perseverance. But for those who are up to the challenge, the rewards can be great. As a solo game developer, you have complete creative control over your project and the freedom to work at your own pace. You also have the opportunity to learn new skills and gain valuable experience that can help you advance your career.

This book is all about helping people who want to make a video game on their own. It goes over all the important steps, from planning and pre-production to actually making the game, and then getting it out into the world through marketing and distribution. We'll talk about the tools and tech you'll need, as well as the challenges and mistakes you might run into along the way. We'll also give you some practical tips and strategies for dealing with those challenges and staying motivated throughout the development process.

Now, let's dive into what you can expect to find in this book. We'll start by talking about the planning and pre-production phase, which is when you take your initial game idea and start to flesh it out, figuring out all the details of how it will work and what it will include. We'll go over how to create a game design document, which is kind of like a blueprint for your game, and how to do some prototyping to test out different ideas and concepts. We'll also talk about setting up your development environment, which refers to all the tools, software, and other resources you'll need to actually build the game.

Next, we'll move on to the production phase, which is when you actually start building your game. We'll cover a variety of topics, like programming and game design, as well as art and audio. We'll also talk about time management and resource management, to help you stay organized and efficient.

After the production phase, we'll delve into marketing and distribution. This is where you'll figure out how to get your game out into the world and into the hands of players. We'll cover topics like building a website and social media presence, creating trailers and other promotional materials, and finding distribution platforms to sell your game. We'll also talk about how to price your game and handle customer support.

Throughout the book, we'll be discussing the tools and technologies you'll need to make your game. These could include game engines, programming languages, art and audio software, and any other specialized tools or assets. We'll also cover the challenges and pitfalls you might encounter during the development process and provide practical tips and strategies for overcoming those challenges and staying motivated.

This book is designed to help aspiring game developers navigate the process of creating a video game completely solo. It covers all the key steps, from planning and pre-production to production, marketing, and distribution. Along the way, we'll discuss the tools and technologies you'll need, as well as the challenges and pitfalls you may encounter. We'll also provide practical tips and strategies for overcoming those challenges and staying motivated throughout the development process.

Our main goal with this book is to help you turn your game development dreams into a reality, no matter if you're just starting out or if you're an experienced developer looking to go it alone.

Whether you're working on a small, personal project or a big commercial release, this book will give you the guidance and motivation you need to make it happen. We'll cover a ton of topics, like game design, prototyping, programming, art, audio, marketing, and distribution. We'll also touch on the business side of game development, like budgeting, contracts, and intellectual property.

Now, let's get into a little more detail about what you can expect to find in this book. We'll start by talking about game design and how to take your initial game idea and start to flesh it out, figuring out all the details of how it will work and what it will include. We'll go over how to create a game design document, which is kind of like a blueprint for your game, and how to do some prototyping to test out different ideas and concepts. We'll also talk about the different tools and technologies you'll need to build your game, like game engines and programming languages.

Next, we'll move on to the production phase, which is when you actually start building your game. We'll cover a variety of topics, like programming and game design, as well as art and audio. We'll also talk about time management and resource management, to help you stay organized and efficient.

After the production phase, we'll delve into marketing and distribution. This is where you'll figure out how to get your game out into the world and into the hands of players. We'll cover topics like building a website and social media presence, creating trailers and other promotional materials, and finding distribution platforms to sell your game. We'll also talk about how to price your game and handle customer support.

Throughout the book, we'll be discussing the business side of game development, including budgets, contracts, and intellectual property. We'll give you practical advice on how to manage these aspects of your project, so you can focus on what you do best: creating an awesome game.

Overall, our goal is to empower you to turn your game development dreams into reality, whether you're a beginner or an experienced developer looking to go it alone. Whether you're working on a small, passion project or a full-fledged commercial release, this book will provide the guidance and inspiration you need to succeed. We'll cover a wide range of topics, including game design, prototyping, programming, art, audio, marketing, and distribution. We'll also discuss the business side of game development, including budgets, contracts, and intellectual property. We hope this book will be a valuable resource for you as you embark on your journey to create your own game.

We want to empower you to achieve your game development dreams, whether you're just starting out or if you're an experienced developer looking to go it alone. This book is here to provide guidance and inspiration, no matter if you're working on a small, personal project or a big commercial release. We'll cover a ton of different topics, from game design and prototyping to programming, art, audio, marketing, and distribution. We'll also delve into the business side of things, like budgeting, contracts, and intellectual property.

We hope this book will be a helpful resource for you as you embark on your journey to create your own game. We want to give you the tools and knowledge you need to succeed, and we're here to support you every step of the way.

By the time you finish this book, you'll have a really good understanding of what it takes to make a video game all by yourself. You'll also have the confidence and skills to turn your own game ideas into a reality. You'll learn how to plan and test out your game, build and fine-tune the mechanics, add art and audio, and get your game out into the world through marketing and distribution. We'll also show you how to troubleshoot problems, get feedback from players, and make any updates your game might need.

By the end of this book, you'll also have a solid understanding of what it takes to create a video game completely solo, as well as the confidence and skills to bring your own game ideas to life. You'll learn how to plan and prototype your game, build and test the mechanics, implement art and audio, and market and distribute your final product. You'll also learn how to troubleshoot problems, gather feedback, and make updates as needed.

There are a ton of benefits to making a video game all by yourself! One of the biggest ones is having complete control over everything. When you're working on a team, sometimes you have to compromise your ideas to make everyone happy. But when you're solo, you get to make every single decision about your game, from the gameplay mechanics to the art and story. This means you can create a game that's totally unique and represents your own style and interests.

Another benefit is being able to work at your own pace. When you're on a team, you might have strict deadlines and schedules to follow. But when you're solo, you can work on your game as much or as little as you want, and take breaks whenever you need them. This is especially helpful for people who have other commitments, like a day job or family stuff to deal with. Working at your own pace can help you balance your game development with everything else in your life and prevent burnout.

Making a game solo can also help you learn new skills! When you're on a team, you might specialize in just one area, like programming or art. But when you're solo, you might have to do a little bit of everything to get your game done. This can be a great opportunity to try out new things and become a more well-rounded developer. Plus, it can help you become more self-sufficient and better able to handle every aspect of game development on your own.

Finally, making a game solo is a great way to gain experience and build a portfolio. Even if your game doesn't become a huge success, the process of creating it from start to finish can be a super valuable learning experience. You can apply what you've learned and show off your skills to potential employers or clients. Plus, by making a game solo, you can get exposure and build a community of fans and supporters. This can be especially helpful for people who are just starting out in the game industry and trying to make a name for themselves.

Overall, making a game solo can be a really rewarding and fulfilling experience. You get complete creative control, the ability to work at your own pace, the chance to learn new skills, and valuable experience. Whether you're a beginner or an experienced developer, there are tons of benefits to making a game solo, and this book is here to help you make the most of them.

As a solo game developer, you may face several challenges that can test your skills and resilience. Some of the common challenges include:

- **Limited resources**: As a solo developer, you may have limited resources at your disposal compared to a larger development team. This may include limited time, money, and access to specialized skills or equipment. You may also have to rely on free or low-cost tools and services, which can have their own limitations and restrictions. These challenges can make it more difficult to develop and polish your game and may require you to be more resourceful and creative in your approach.

- **Wearing multiple hats**: As a solo developer, you may need to handle every aspect of game development on your own, from programming and design to art and audio. This can be a lot of work and may require you to learn new skills or stretch your existing skills in new ways. You may also need to juggle multiple tasks and responsibilities at once, which can be challenging and time-consuming. To succeed as a solo developer, you'll need to be able to manage your workload effectively and stay organized.

- **Limited feedback and support**: When you're working on a team, you have the benefit of receiving feedback and support from your colleagues. But as a solo developer, you may have to rely on friends, family, or online communities for feedback and support. This can be more difficult and time-consuming and may not be as effective as getting feedback from professionals or experienced developers. You may also have to work harder to get noticed and build a community of supporters.

- **Limited exposure and marketing resources**: As a solo developer, you may have limited resources for marketing and promoting your game. This can make it more difficult to get your game noticed and attract a large audience. You may have to rely on social media, online communities, and other low-cost marketing methods to get the word out about your game. You may also have to compete with larger, more established developers for attention.

- **Legal and financial challenges**: As a solo developer, you may have to handle the legal and financial aspects of game development on your own. This can include negotiating contracts, dealing with intellectual property issues, and managing budgets and expenses. These tasks can be complex and time-consuming and may require you to seek legal or financial advice from professionals.

- **Burnout and isolation**: Working on a game solo can be a rewarding and fulfilling experience, but it can also be isolating and stressful. You may have to work long hours and handle every aspect of game development on your own, which can lead to burnout and fatigue. It's important to take breaks, get enough rest, and maintain a healthy work-life balance. You may also need to find ways to stay motivated and connected to others, such as joining online communities or collaborating with other developers.

Being a solo game developer can definitely be tough, but it can also be super rewarding and fulfilling. To succeed, you'll need to be resourceful, organized, and resilient. You'll also need to be able to manage your workload and stay motivated. Plus, you'll need to figure out how to handle the legal and financial stuff and find ways to get feedback and support. But if you're aware of these challenges and come up with strategies to overcome them, you can create an awesome game and enjoy the process of making it.

Whether you're just starting out as a game developer, doing it as a hobby, or if you're an experienced developer looking to go it alone, we hope this book will give you the guidance and inspiration you need to succeed. We'll cover a ton of different topics, from game design and prototyping to programming, art, audio, marketing, and distribution. We'll also talk about the business side of things, like budgeting, contracts, and intellectual property.

So, if you're ready to start your solo game development journey, let's get going! We believe that anyone can create a great video game with the right tools, guidance, and determination. Whether you're a beginner or an experienced developer, join us on this journey and let's make your dream game together!

Chapter 2:

Planning and Pre-Production

Introduction

Hey there! We're so glad you're joining us for the Planning and Preproduction chapter. If you're new to game development, you might be wondering why planning and preproduction are so important.

The truth is, they play a crucial role in the success of any game development project. By taking the time to properly plan and prepare, you can save yourself a lot of time, effort, and resources in the long run. Not only that, but you'll also increase your chances of success and avoid common pitfalls and setbacks. So, it's definitely worth investing the time and energy into planning and preproduction.

So, what exactly does planning and preproduction involve? There are a few key steps and techniques that we'll be covering. First off, you'll need to define your game idea. This is where you get to brainstorm and come up with creative ideas for your game. You'll need to answer questions like: What's the core concept of your game? What are the gameplay mechanics and features? Who is your target audience and market? What makes your game unique and compelling?

There are lots of ways to brainstorm and generate ideas for your game. You could try using techniques like mind maps, word association, or even just a pen and paper. You could also look at other games or media for inspiration. Just remember to keep an open mind and be willing to try new things.

Once you have a solid game idea, you'll need to identify your target audience and market. This will help you determine the right genre, style, and tone for your game and help you tailor your marketing and distribution efforts. For example, if your target audience is casual gamers, you might want to consider creating a mobile game or a simple puzzle game. If your target audience is hardcore gamers, you might want to consider creating a more complex or immersive experience.

To choose a game genre and style that fits your game idea and your target audience, you'll need to consider the art style, tone, and overall aesthetic of your game. Will your game be 2D or

3D? Will it be realistic or stylized? Will it be set in a fantasy world or a modern-day setting? These are all important questions to consider.

Next, we'll talk about creating a game design document (GDD). A GDD is basically a blueprint for your game. It outlines all the key components and features of your game, like the concept, gameplay mechanics, levels, art style, audio, and story. A well-written GDD can help you communicate your vision and goals to your team (if you have one) and serve as a reference guide throughout the development process.

After that, we'll delve into the topic of prototyping and testing your game. Prototyping is the process of creating a simplified or experimental version of your game to validate and refine your ideas. It's a crucial step that can save you a lot of time and effort in the long run, by helping you identify and fix any issues early on. Prototyping can take many forms, like paper prototypes, digital prototypes, or even physical prototypes. The goal of prototyping is to test your ideas and mechanics and identify and fix any issues before you invest too much time and effort into the final game.

Next, we'll look at setting up your development environment. This involves choosing the right tools and platforms for your game and setting up your project folder and development environment. You'll also want to consider any third-party assets or resources that you'll need, like music or sound effects.

Next, we'll discuss preproduction tasks like creating a project schedule, budgeting, and assembling your team (if you have one). A project schedule is a timeline that outlines all the tasks and milestones for your game development project. It's a great way to stay organized and on track, and it can help you identify any potential issues or bottlenecks.

Budgeting involves estimating the cost of your project and allocating resources accordingly, and it's an important step to ensure that you have the necessary resources to complete your project. If you have a team, you'll need to assemble the right people and establish clear roles and responsibilities.

Assembling your team is an important part of preproduction. You'll want to consider the skills and expertise that you need for your project and find people who are the right fit for your team. This might include programmers, artists, designers, writers, and more. Depending on the size and scope of your project, you might have a large team or a small team. Either way, it's important to have a clear communication plan in place and to establish roles and responsibilities for each member of the team.

Once you have your game idea, GDD, and team in place, you'll be ready to start the actual production phase. But before you dive in, it's important to make sure that you have all the necessary resources and support in place. This might include funding, equipment, software licenses, and more. It's also a good idea to set up a project management system to keep track of tasks, deadlines, and progress.

So that's it for the Planning and Preproduction chapter! We hope you feel more prepared and confident about planning and preparing for your game development project. Remember to take your time, be organized, and don't be afraid to ask for help or resources if you need them. Good luck and have fun!

Defining your game idea

Defining your game idea is an important step in the game development process, and it's one that should not be rushed. This is where you get to brainstorm and come up with creative ideas for your game, and it's an opportunity to really let your imagination run wild. It's also an important step that will set the direction for your project, so it's worth investing the time and effort to do it right. In this section, we'll be discussing the importance of defining your game idea and covering some key techniques for brainstorming and generating ideas. Whether you're a solo developer or part of a team, these techniques can help you come up with unique and compelling game ideas that stand out in the market.

There are a few key questions you'll want to answer as you define your game idea: What is the core concept of your game? What are the gameplay mechanics and features? Who is your target audience and market? What makes your game unique and compelling?

There are many different techniques you can use to brainstorm and generate ideas for your game. One popular method is mind mapping, which involves creating a visual representation of your ideas by drawing a central concept and then branching out with related ideas. This can be a great way to organize your thoughts and see the big picture, as well as to identify any gaps or areas that need further exploration. To create a mind map, you can start by drawing a circle in the middle of a blank page and writing your central concept inside. Then, you can draw lines emanating from the centre and write related ideas on branches coming off of those lines. You can also use different colours or symbols to differentiate between different types of ideas or to highlight particularly important ideas.

Another technique you might try is word association, where you start with a key word or phrase and then come up with as many related words or phrases as you can. This can be a great way to spark new ideas and get your creative juices flowing. To use this technique, you can start by writing your key word or phrase in the centre of a blank page and then jotting down as many related words or phrases as you can think of around it. You can also try using a word generator tool or thesaurus to come up with new ideas.

In addition to these techniques, you might find it helpful to look at other games or media for inspiration, or to take a break and do something else for a while to let your ideas marinate. It's often said that "creativity loves constraints," so you might want to set yourself some boundaries or parameters to work within. For example, you might decide to come up with a game idea that fits within a specific genre or that utilizes a particular gameplay mechanic. Whatever method you choose, it's important to keep an open mind and be willing to try new things. The more you practice brainstorming and idea generation, the better you'll become at it.

Once you have a solid game idea, it's time to start thinking about your target audience and market. This is an important step that will help you determine the right genre, style, and tone for your game, as well as tailor your marketing and distribution efforts. Identifying your target audience and market is all about understanding who your game is for and what they are looking for in a game.

There are many different factors to consider when identifying your target audience and market. For example, you'll want to think about the age range of your target audience, their interests and hobbies, their level of experience with games, and their preferred platforms. You'll also want to think about the type of game you're creating and what makes it unique and compelling. All of these factors will help you determine the right genre, style, and tone for your game.

For example, if your target audience is casual gamers, you might want to consider creating a mobile game or a simple puzzle game that can be played in short bursts. If your target audience is hardcore gamers, you might want to consider creating a more complex or immersive experience that offers a deeper level of challenge and engagement. Whatever your target audience and market, it's important to keep them in mind as you develop your game and plan your marketing and distribution efforts. By understanding your target audience and market, you can create a game that resonates with them and meets their needs.

Finally, you'll need to choose a game genre and style that fits your game idea and your target audience. This is an important step that will help you determine the direction of your project and ensure that you're creating a game that resonates with your audience. There are many different game genres to choose from, including action, adventure, role-playing, strategy, and more. Each genre has its own set of conventions and expectations, and it's important to choose a genre that fits your game idea and your target audience.

In addition to choosing a genre, you'll also need to consider the art style, tone, and overall aesthetic of your game. Will your game be 2D or 3D? Will it be realistic or stylized? Will it be set in a fantasy world or a modern-day setting? These are all important questions to consider as you define your game idea. The choices you make at this stage will have a big impact on the direction of your project, so it's important to give them careful thought.

There are no right or wrong answers to these questions, and the best choice will depend on your game idea, your target audience, and your personal preferences. It's important to be true to yourself and your vision, but at the same time, you'll want to ensure that your game is feasible and marketable. By taking the time to carefully consider your game genre, style, and aesthetic, you can create a game that stands out in the market and resonates with your target audience.

Identifying your target audience and market

In this section, we'll be discussing the importance of identifying your target audience and market.

Before you can start developing your game, it's important to consider who your game is for. Who is your target audience? What are their interests and preferences? What are their motivations for playing games? Understanding your target audience is crucial to the success of your game, as it will help you create a game that resonates with them and meets their needs.

There are many different factors to consider when identifying your target audience. For example, you'll want to think about the age range of your target audience, their interests and hobbies, their level of experience with games, and their preferred platforms. You'll also want to think about the type of game you're creating and what makes it unique and compelling. All of these factors will help you determine the right genre, style, and tone for your game, and they'll help you tailor your marketing and distribution efforts to your target audience.

Understanding your target audience can also help you identify potential challenges and opportunities. For example, if your target audience is primarily made up of younger players, you might want to consider incorporating educational or learning elements into your game. If your target audience is primarily made up of experienced gamers, you might want to consider offering a high level of challenge or depth. Whatever your target audience, it's important to keep them in mind as you develop your game and plan your marketing and distribution efforts. By understanding your target audience, you can create a game that resonates with them and meets their needs.

One way to identify your target audience is to create a persona, or a fictional character that represents your ideal player. A persona can help you visualize who your game is for, and it can help you make design and development decisions that cater to their interests and preferences. By creating a persona, you can gain a better understanding of your target audience and how they might engage with your game.

To create a persona, you'll want to consider factors such as age, gender, interests, hobbies, motivations, and experience with games. You can use this information to create a detailed profile of your ideal player, complete with a name, a photograph, and a brief description of their personality and characteristics. You might even want to create a backstory or a "day in the life" scenario to help you understand how your persona would interact with your game.

For example, if your persona is a casual gamer who enjoys puzzle games on their mobile device, you might want to consider creating a mobile puzzle game. This persona might be a busy working parent who enjoys playing games on their phone during their commute or during breaks at work. They might be looking for a game that is easy to pick up and play, but that still offers a satisfying level of challenge and progression. By understanding your persona's interests, preferences, and motivations, you can create a game that resonates with them and meets their needs.

In addition to identifying your target audience, you'll also need to consider what platform or devices they will be using to play your game. Different platforms and devices have different hardware and software requirements, and it's important to choose the right one for your game. This will help ensure that your game runs smoothly and performs well on the chosen platform, and it will help you reach your target audience.

For example, if your game is a PC game, you'll need to consider the hardware and operating system requirements for PC gamers. You'll want to make sure that your game can run on the most common hardware configurations and operating systems, and you'll want to test your game on a variety of different systems to ensure compatibility. You'll also want to consider the distribution platform for your PC game, such as Steam or Epic Games Store.

If your game is a mobile game, you'll need to consider the hardware and operating system requirements for mobile devices. You'll want to make sure that your game can run on the most common mobile devices and operating systems, and you'll want to test your game on a variety of different devices to ensure compatibility. You'll also want to consider the distribution platform for your mobile game, such as the App Store or Google Play.

Regardless of the platform or device you choose, it's important to consider the hardware and software requirements early in the development process. This will help you avoid any compatibility issues or performance issues down the line, and it will help you reach your target audience.

Another important factor to consider when planning your game is the demand for games like yours on the market. Is there a demand for your game genre, style, and theme? What are the trends in the gaming industry, and how can you capitalize on them? It's important to do market research and stay up to date on industry trends to ensure that your game will be successful.

There are a few different ways you can do market research for your game. One way is to look at sales data for similar games and see how they have performed in the market. This can help you get a sense of the demand for games like yours, and it can help you identify any potential challenges or opportunities. You can also look at reviews and player feedback for similar games to see what people like and dislike about them, and you can use this information to inform your own game development.

Another way to do market research is to look at industry trends and see how you can capitalize on them. For example, if you notice that there is a trend towards games with strong storytelling and characters, you might want to consider incorporating these elements into your game. If you notice that there is a trend towards games with multiplayer modes, you might want to consider adding a multiplayer mode to your game. By staying up to date on industry trends, you can ensure that your game is relevant and appealing to your target audience.

Overall, it's important to do market research and stay up to date on industry trends to ensure that your game will be successful. By understanding the demand for games like yours and staying current on industry trends, you can create a game that resonates with your target audience and meets their needs.

Choosing a game genre and style

In this section, we'll be discussing the importance of choosing a game genre and style that fits your game idea and your target audience.

When it comes to choosing a game genre, there are many different options to consider. Some popular game genres include action, adventure, role-playing, strategy, and more. Each genre has its own unique characteristics and conventions, and it's important to choose the one that best fits your game idea and your target audience.

For example, if you're creating a game that involves a lot of combat and fast-paced action, you might want to consider the action genre. This genre is known for its high-energy gameplay and intense challenges, and it's often popular with players who enjoy adrenaline-fueled experiences. Action games can be 2D or 3D, and they can take place in a variety of settings, including futuristic worlds, historical periods, or fantasy realms. Some popular sub-genres of action games include first-person shooters, platformers, and fighting games.

On the other hand, if you're creating a game that involves a lot of exploration, puzzles, and storytelling, you might want to consider the adventure genre. This genre is known for its immersive worlds and engaging narratives, and it's often popular with players who enjoy immersive and atmospheric experiences. Adventure games can be 2D or 3D, and they can take place in a variety of settings, including realistic worlds, fantasy realms, or historical periods. Some popular sub-genres of adventure games include role-playing games, point-and-click games, and visual novels.

In addition to choosing a game genre, you'll also need to consider the art style and theme of your game. The art style refers to the visual aesthetic of your game, including the overall look and feel of the graphics, characters, and environments. The art style can be realistic, stylized, or somewhere in between, and it can be 2D or 3D. Some popular art styles include pixel art, hand-drawn animation, and 3D modelling.

The theme refers to the underlying message or concept of your game, such as a historical setting, a fantasy world, or a futuristic world. The theme can be serious, light-hearted, or somewhere in between, and it can be based on real-world events or completely fictional. Some popular themes for games include science fiction, fantasy, and horror.

The art style and theme of your game should complement each other and support the overall concept and gameplay of your game. For example, if your game is a fantasy role-playing game, you might want to consider a stylized art style and a fantasy theme. If your game is a realistic first-person shooter, you might want to consider a realistic art style and a modern-day or futuristic theme.

When choosing the art style and theme of your game, it's important to consider the preferences of your target audience. Your target audience can vary in age, gender, culture, and interests, and it's important to understand what they like and dislike when it comes to the visual and conceptual aspects of a game.

For example, if your target audience is young children, you might want to consider using a more cartoony and colourful art style. Children tend to be attracted to bright, vibrant colours and simple, exaggerated shapes, and a cartoony art style can help capture their attention and imagination. On the other hand, if your target audience is older teens or adults, you might want to consider using a more realistic or stylized art style. Teens and adults tend to be more discerning when it comes to graphics and aesthetics, and they may appreciate a more detailed or stylized art style.

The theme of your game should also be consistent with your target audience and the genre of your game. For example, if you're creating a fantasy role-playing game, you might want to consider using a fantasy theme. This theme can help create an immersive and atmospheric world that resonates with players who enjoy fantasy and role-playing games. On the other hand, if you're creating a science fiction action game, you might want to consider using a science fiction theme. This theme can help create a futuristic and technologically advanced world that resonates with players who enjoy science fiction and action games.

Overall, it's important to choose an art style and theme that fit your game idea and your target audience, and that support the overall concept and gameplay of your game. By choosing the right art style and theme for your game, you can create a visually appealing and immersive experience that resonates with your target audience and meets their needs.

Creating a game design document

In this section, we'll be discussing the importance of creating a game design document (GDD) and we'll be covering some key techniques for writing a clear and concise GDD.

But first, let's start with the basics: What is a game design document (GDD)? A GDD is a comprehensive document that outlines the design and vision for your game. It serves as a blueprint for your game development process, and it helps you stay organized, focused, and efficient. A GDD typically includes details about the game concept, gameplay mechanics, levels, art style, audio, and story, as well as any other key components and features of your game.

A GDD can also be used to communicate your ideas and plans to other members of your development team, as well as to potential investors, partners, and publishers. It's a useful tool for getting everyone on the same page and ensuring that everyone is working towards the same goals. A GDD can also help you track your progress and identify any issues or roadblocks that may arise during the development process.

Creating a GDD can be a time-consuming and challenging task, but it's well worth the effort. A well-written GDD can help you clarify your vision and goals for your game, and it can help you stay focused and organized as you bring your game to life. It can also serve as a valuable reference guide throughout the development process, and it can help you communicate your ideas effectively to others.

A GDD is an essential tool for any game development project, and it's an important step in the planning and preproduction process. By taking the time to create a comprehensive and well-written GDD, you can set yourself up for success and increase your chances of creating a successful game.

So, how do you create a GDD? There's no one-size-fits-all formula for creating a GDD, as it will depend on your game idea, your target audience, and your development goals. However, there are some general guidelines you can follow to create a GDD that is clear, concise, and effective.

First and foremost, it's important to be thorough and comprehensive. A GDD should cover all the key aspects and features of your game, and it should provide enough detail to give a clear and accurate picture of your vision. This means including things like the game concept, gameplay mechanics, levels, art style, audio, and story, as well as any other important details that help to define your game.

It's also important to be organized and structured. A GDD should be easy to read and understand, and it should be organized in a logical and coherent way. This might involve using headings, subheadings, bullet points, or other formatting tools to help break up the text and make it more readable.

Finally, it's important to be clear and concise. A GDD should get to the point and avoid unnecessary or extraneous information. This means avoiding jargon, technical language, or ambiguous terms, and it means focusing on the most important details and leaving out anything that isn't essential.

Overall, creating a GDD is a crucial step in the planning and preproduction process, and it's an opportunity to clarify your vision and goals for your game. By following these general guidelines, you can create a GDD that is clear, concise, and effective, and that helps you stay organized and focused throughout the development process.

First, start by brainstorming and organizing your ideas. This is where you get to come up with creative and innovative ideas for your game. Think about the core gameplay mechanics, the characters, the storyline, the levels, the art style, the audio, and any other key elements of your game. Write down your ideas and organize them into categories or sections.

There are many ways to brainstorm and organize your ideas. You might try using mind maps, word association, or other creative thinking techniques to generate new ideas and connections. You might also find it helpful to look at other games or media for inspiration, or to get feedback from friends, family, or other stakeholders.

Whatever method you choose, it's important to be open to new ideas and to think outside the box. Don't be afraid to take risks and try new things and be willing to be flexible and adapt your ideas as needed. By taking the time to brainstorm and organize your ideas, you can create a solid foundation for your game design and set yourself up for success.

Next, define the scope of your game. This is where you get to think about what you want to achieve with your game and how you're going to get there. What are your goals and objectives? What are the key features and elements of your game that will help you reach those goals? Defining the scope of your game is an important step that helps you stay focused and avoid scope creep, which is when a project becomes larger and more complex than originally intended.

Scope creep can be a big problem in game development, as it can lead to delays, budget overruns, and other issues. By defining the scope of your game upfront, you can set clear boundaries and expectations for what's included in your game and what's not. This will help you stay on track and avoid wasting time and resources on features that aren't essential to your game.

To define the scope of your game, it's helpful to create a list of must-have and nice-to-have features. Must-have features are the essential elements that are necessary for your game to function and be enjoyable. Nice-to-have features are the optional or extra elements that would be nice to have but aren't essential. By prioritizing your features and being clear about what's included in your game, you can make informed decisions about your development efforts and stay within your scope.

Once you have a clear idea of your game and its scope, you can start writing your GDD. A GDD typically includes several sections that outline the key components and features of your game, such as a concept section, a gameplay mechanics section, a levels section, an art style section, an audio section, and a story section. Depending on your game, you might also want to include other sections, such as a controls section, a character design section, a world design section, or a technical requirements section.

Each section of your GDD should be written in a clear and concise manner, and it should include specific details and examples to illustrate your ideas. For example, in the concept section, you might want to describe the core concept of your game, the gameplay mechanics and features, the target audience and market, and what makes your game unique and compelling. In the gameplay mechanics section, you might want to describe how your game plays, including the controls, the player actions, the enemies, and the objectives. In the levels section, you might want to describe the different levels or environments in your game, including the layout, the challenges, and the progression.

Writing a GDD can be a lot of work, but it's an important step in the game development process. A well-written GDD can help you communicate your vision and goals to your team and stakeholders, and it can serve as a reference guide throughout the development process. It's also a great way to solidify your ideas and make sure that you have a clear plan before you start developing your game.

It's also important to include a timeline or schedule in your GDD. A timeline will help you plan and coordinate your development process, and it will help you track your progress and meet your deadlines. Creating a timeline involves breaking down your development process into smaller, more manageable tasks and estimating how long each task will take. This can help you identify bottlenecks and potential roadblocks, and it can help you allocate your resources and manpower more effectively.

Your timeline should be realistic and achievable, and it should allow for some flexibility and contingency. It's also a good idea to include milestones in your timeline, which are key events or achievements that mark significant progress in your development process. Milestones can help you stay motivated and on track, and they can also help you celebrate your achievements along the way.

In addition to a timeline, you might also want to include a budget in your GDD. A budget will help you plan and manage your financial resources, and it will help you make informed decisions about your project. A budget can include a variety of costs, such as development costs, marketing costs, distribution costs, and more. It's important to be as accurate and detailed as possible when creating a budget, as it will help you stay on track and avoid overspending.

Finally, review and revise your GDD. Once you've completed your GDD, it's important to review it and make any necessary revisions. This is your chance to ensure that your GDD is accurate, comprehensive, and coherent, and that it reflects your vision and goals for your game.

Start by checking for spelling and grammar errors. A GDD is a professional document, and it's important to present it in the best light possible. You might also want to consider the tone and style of your GDD, and make sure that it's clear and easy to understand. Use simple, concise language, and avoid using jargon or technical terms that might be confusing to your audience.

You might also want to ask other members of your development team or trusted colleagues to review your GDD and provide feedback. Their perspective can be valuable, as they might spot errors or areas for improvement that you might have missed. Be open to feedback and be willing to make revisions as needed.

Overall, the review and revision process is an important step in the game development process, and it can help you create a GDD that is accurate, coherent, and effective.

If you're looking for examples of game design documents, there are various ones available online that you can use as a reference or guide.

Prototyping And Testing Your Game

In this section, we'll be discussing the importance of prototyping and testing your game, and we'll be covering some key techniques for prototyping and testing.

But first, let's start with the basics: What is prototyping? Prototyping is the process of creating a simplified version of your game in order to test and validate your ideas. It allows you to experiment with different gameplay mechanics, levels, art styles, and other key elements of your game, and it helps you identify and fix any issues or problems before you invest a lot of time and resources into the final version of your game.

You may have heard the term 'vertical slice' in the context of game development. But what exactly is a vertical slice, and why is it important?

A vertical slice is a representative version of your game that showcases key features and gameplay mechanics. It's called a "vertical slice" because it represents a slice or cross-section of your game, rather than the entire game. A vertical slice is typically developed early in the game development process, and it serves as a prototype for your game.

The purpose of a vertical slice is to demonstrate the vision and potential of your game to stakeholders, such as investors, partners, and publishers. It allows you to show off your game's core gameplay, art style, audio, and other key features, and it gives stakeholders a sense of what your game will be like.

A vertical slice is also a useful tool for testing and validating your game ideas. It allows you to playtest your game and gather feedback from players and testers, and it helps you identify and fix any issues or problems. This can save you time and resources in the long run, and it can help you create a better and more enjoyable game.

Prototyping is an essential part of the game development process, and it can help you save time, money, and effort in the long run. It's also a great way to get feedback from your players and testers, and it can help you improve the overall quality and enjoyment of your game.

So, how do you prototype your game? There are several approaches to prototyping, and the right approach will depend on your game idea, your resources, and your goals. Here are some common techniques for prototyping your game:

- **Paper prototyping**: Paper prototyping is a technique used in game development to quickly create a physical or digital representation of a game using paper, pencils, and other basic materials. The purpose of paper prototyping is to test and validate game ideas, mechanics, levels, and other key elements of a game without investing a lot of time and resources into the final version of the game.

Paper prototyping is a simple and inexpensive way to get a sense of how a game will play and feel, and it can be a great starting point for the development process. It allows developers to experiment with different ideas and mechanics, and it can help identify and fix any issues or problems early on.

To create a paper prototype, developers typically sketch out the gameplay mechanics, levels, and other elements of the game on paper or digitally. They can then playtest the prototype with friends or colleagues to get feedback and identify any issues or problems. Paper prototyping is a flexible and iterative process, and developers may need to revise and update their prototypes based on playtesting results.

- **Digital prototyping**: Digital prototyping is the process of creating a digital version of a product or system in order to test and validate its functionality, design, and user experience. In the context of game development, digital prototyping involves creating a basic version of a game using game development software or other specialized tools.

The goal of digital prototyping is to quickly and inexpensively test and refine the key elements of a game, such as gameplay mechanics, levels, art style, and audio. It allows developers to experiment with different ideas and approaches, and it helps them identify and fix any issues or problems before investing a lot of time and resources into the final version of the game.

Digital prototyping is a crucial part of the game development process, as it helps developers ensure that their game is fun, engaging, and feasible to develop. It also allows developers to get feedback from players and testers, and it helps them improve the overall quality and enjoyment of their game.

To create a digital prototype, developers typically use game development software such as Unity or Unreal Engine, or specialized prototyping tools such as InVision or Marvel. These tools provide a range of features and capabilities, including 3D modelling, animation, physics, audio, and more, which allow developers to create a realistic and interactive version of their game.

Digital prototyping can be a time-consuming and technical process, and it requires a certain level of skill and knowledge. However, it can greatly benefit the game development process by providing a clear and efficient way to test and refine the key elements of a game.

- **Hybrid prototyping**: Hybrid prototyping is a combination of paper prototyping and digital prototyping techniques. It involves creating a physical or digital version of your game using a combination of paper, pencils, and other basic materials, as well as game development software or other specialized tools. The goal of hybrid prototyping is to take advantage of the strengths of both paper prototyping and digital prototyping, and to create a flexible and efficient prototyping process.

Paper prototyping is a simple and inexpensive way to test your game ideas, and it allows you to quickly sketch out your gameplay mechanics, levels, and other key elements of your game. Digital prototyping, on the other hand, is a more advanced and time-consuming approach, and it requires more technical skills and resources. By combining the two, you can create a basic paper prototype to test your ideas, and then use digital tools to create a more advanced version of your prototype.

Hybrid prototyping can be particularly useful in game development, as it allows you to test and iterate on your game ideas quickly and efficiently. It also allows you to playtest your game with a wider range of players, and to get feedback on your game mechanics, levels, and other elements. Overall, hybrid prototyping is a flexible and efficient approach that can help you save time, money, and effort in the game development process.

Prototyping is an ongoing process, and it's important to be open to iteration and change. As you prototype and playtest your game, you'll likely discover new ideas, features, and improvements that you hadn't thought of before. You may also encounter issues or problems that you hadn't anticipated, and you'll need to adapt and revise your prototype accordingly. This is why it's important to approach prototyping with an open mind and a flexible attitude.

Don't be afraid to try new things and make changes to your prototype, even if it means starting over from scratch.

The more you prototype and playtest your game, the better it will become. It's also important to keep track of your progress and document any changes or updates to your prototype. This will help you stay organized and focused, and it will make it easier to communicate your ideas to your team and stakeholders. Additionally, you might need to update your game design document (GDD) based on your prototyping results. Your GDD should be a living document that reflects the current state of your game, and it's important to keep it up-to-date as you prototype and iterate on your game.

Setting up your development environment

In this section, we'll be discussing the importance of setting up your development environment, and we'll be covering some key techniques for staying organized and efficient.

A development environment is an essential aspect of the game development process, as it serves as the place where you'll be spending most of your time creating and testing your game. A good development environment should be tailored to your specific needs and preferences and should provide you with everything you need to bring your game to life. This includes the necessary hardware, software, and tools, as well as a comfortable and inspiring space to work in. A development environment can be a physical space, such as a dedicated room or office, or it can be a virtual space, such as a cloud-based platform or software. In either case, it's important to choose the right tools and resources to support your development process, and to create an environment that is conducive to productivity and creativity. Whether you're working alone or with a team, a well-organized and efficient development environment is key to the success of your game.

So, how do you set up your development environment? Here are some tips to help you get started:

First, you'll need to choose the right tools and software for your game. This will depend on your game idea and your goals, as well as your budget and technical skills. Some common tools and software for game development include game engines, programming languages, art and audio software, and project management tools. Do your research and take the time to evaluate different options before making a decision. Consider factors such as compatibility, features, performance, and user reviews. You may also want to consider free or open-source alternatives, as they can save you money and offer a wide range of options and resources.

Once you've chosen your tools and software, you'll need to create a project folder to store and organize all your game assets, files, and documents. A project folder is essentially a virtual workspace that helps you keep track of your progress and resources. Use a consistent naming convention and file structure and consider using version control or asset management tools to help you manage your assets. This will save you time and effort and prevent errors or confusion.

Your workstation is another important aspect of your development environment. This is the place where you'll be spending most of your time working on your game, so it's essential that it's comfortable, ergonomic, and well-equipped. Invest in a good chair, monitor, keyboard, and mouse, and make sure you have enough light, ventilation, and space to work comfortably. A cluttered or poorly equipped workstation can lead to poor posture, eyestrain, fatigue, and decreased productivity, so it's worth taking the time to set it up properly.

Finally, you'll need to manage your time and resources effectively to stay on track and avoid burnout. Game development can be a complex and time-consuming process, so it's important to set clear goals and deadlines, and prioritize your tasks based on their importance and complexity. Use productivity techniques, such as the Pomodoro Technique or the 80/20 rule, to focus and optimize your work. Take breaks, stay hydrated, and avoid distractions as much as possible. It's also a good idea to set aside time for self-care, such as exercise, socializing, or hobbies, to keep your mind and body healthy and balanced.

Conclusion

Congratulations on reaching the conclusion of Chapter 2: Planning and Preproduction! This chapter has covered some of the most important steps and techniques for planning and preproduction in game development, and it's crucial to understand these concepts in order to be successful in the game development process.

In this chapter, we've learned about the importance of defining your game idea. This involves brainstorming and idea generation, as well as identifying your target audience and market. Once you have a clear idea of what your game is going to be and who it's for, you can move on to choosing a game genre and style. This involves deciding on the type of game you want to create, as well as the art style and theme that will be used.

Another important step in planning and preproduction is creating a game design document. This document serves as a blueprint for your game, outlining all the key aspects of gameplay, mechanics, levels, and other features. It's essential to have a game design document in place, as it helps you stay organized and focused, and it ensures that you have a clear roadmap for development.

Prototyping and testing your game is another crucial step in the planning and preproduction phase. Prototyping involves creating a rough version of your game in order to test out gameplay mechanics and other features. This allows you to get a sense of how your game will play and feel, and it allows you to make any necessary changes or adjustments before you get too far into development.

Finally, setting up your development environment is an important part of the planning and preproduction process. A development environment is the place where you'll be creating and testing your game, and it should be comfortable, productive, and well-equipped to support your needs. This involves choosing the right tools and software, creating a project folder, setting up your workstation, and managing your time and resources effectively.

Throughout this chapter, we've covered a range of topics and techniques that are essential for planning and preproduction in game development. We've learned about the importance of defining your game idea, identifying your target audience and market, choosing a game genre and style, creating a game design document, prototyping and testing your game, and setting up your development environment. We've also explored the importance of managing your time and resources, and we've discussed some key strategies for staying organized and efficient.

Now, let's take a moment to reflect on why planning and preproduction are so important in game development. Simply put, planning and preproduction are critical to the success of your game. They help you clarify your vision, align your goals, and allocate your resources in the most effective way. They also help you avoid common pitfalls and setbacks, and they enable you to create a more engaging, polished, and profitable game.

So, what comes next in the game development process? Once you've completed your planning and preproduction phase, you'll be ready to move on to the production phase. This is where you'll be building and testing your game mechanics and levels, implementing your art, audio, and other assets, and debugging and fixing issues as they arise. After that, you'll be ready to move on to the marketing and distribution phase, where you'll be creating a marketing plan, building a website and social media presence, releasing your game on various platforms, and gathering feedback and making updates.

But this is just the beginning! As a solo game developer, you'll be constantly learning, adapting, and growing, and there will always be new challenges and opportunities ahead. So stay focused, stay motivated, and don't be afraid to seek help or advice when you need it. With hard work, dedication, and passion, you can create a game that will be enjoyed by players all around the world. And don't forget to have fun along the way! Game development can be a rewarding and fulfilling journey, and it's important to enjoy the process as much as the end result.

Chapter 3:
Production

Introduction

Welcome to Chapter 3: Production! In this section, we'll be exploring the importance of the production phase in game development, and we'll be introducing some of the key skills and abilities that are necessary for successful production.

So, why is the production phase important in game development? Simply put, the production phase is where you'll be building and refining your game. It's where you'll be taking all of the ideas, concepts, and plans that you've created in the planning and preproduction phase, and you'll be turning them into a functional, enjoyable, and complete game. This is a crucial and challenging stage of game development, and it requires a wide range of skills and abilities, including problem-solving, creativity, attention to detail, and the ability to work well under pressure.

So, what are the skills and abilities required for successful production? In order to be successful in the production phase, you'll need to have a strong foundation in various technical and artistic disciplines. This may include programming, art, audio, design, and other areas, depending on the nature and scope of your game. You'll also need to be able to work effectively as part of a team, communicate clearly and effectively, and manage your time and resources effectively. Finally, you'll need to be able to adapt to change, handle setbacks and challenges, and stay motivated and focused throughout the development process.

In the following sections, we'll be diving into more detail about the specific tasks and techniques that you'll need to master in order to succeed in the production phase. We'll be covering topics such as choosing the right tools and technologies, building and testing the game mechanics and levels, implementing art, audio, and other assets, and debugging and fixing issues as they arise.

One important aspect of the production phase is the ability to effectively manage your time and resources. This can be especially challenging for game developers, as games are complex and multifaceted projects that require the coordination of many different disciplines and individuals. A good project manager is able to create a realistic and flexible schedule that takes into account the needs and dependencies of different team members and is able to adjust the schedule as needed to accommodate changes or unforeseen challenges.

Another important skill during the production phase is the ability to debug and fix issues as they arise. No matter how well you plan and prepare, there will always be issues and problems that need to be addressed during the development process. A good game developer is able to identify the root cause of an issue and is able to come up with creative and effective solutions to fix it. This requires a combination of technical expertise, problem-solving skills, and attention to detail.

Effective communication is also essential during the production phase. As a game developer, you'll be working with a variety of different people, including programmers, artists, audio designers, testers, and producers. It's important to be able to communicate your ideas and needs clearly and effectively, and to be able to listen and respond to the feedback and concerns of others. This can be achieved through a variety of methods, including face-to-face meetings, online communication tools, and written documentation.

In addition to these general skills, there are many other specific tasks and techniques that are important during the production phase. For example, you'll need to choose the right tools and technologies to create your game, and you'll need to build and test the game mechanics and levels to ensure that they are fun, engaging, and balanced. You'll also need to implement art, audio, and other assets, and you'll need to ensure that they are of high quality and are consistent with the overall vision of your game.

Whether you're an aspiring game developer or an experienced professional branching out on their own, we hope that this chapter will provide you with the knowledge and skills that you need to create a truly great game.

Building and refining game mechanics

Building and refining gameplay mechanics is a crucial part of the production phase of game development, especially when working solo. Gameplay mechanics are the core rules and systems that define how a player interacts with the game. These mechanics can include things like character movement, combat, puzzles, and progression systems. As a solo game developer, it's important to carefully consider and plan out these mechanics in order to create a cohesive and enjoyable game.

Before diving into the implementation of gameplay mechanics, it's important to first decide on the mechanics you want to include in your game. This can involve brainstorming and sketching out ideas, as well as researching similar games to see what mechanics have been successful. It's also important to consider the theme and tone of your game, as well as the target audience, in order to choose mechanics that fit well with the overall vision of your game.

Once you have a clear idea of the gameplay mechanics you want to include, the next step is to start implementing and testing them. This can involve using a game engine or other software to create a rough version of the mechanics and playtest them. It's important to gather as much feedback as possible from playtesters, as this will help you identify any issues or problems with the mechanics and make necessary changes.

Iterating and refining gameplay mechanics is an ongoing process that should be repeated throughout the production phase. As players test the mechanics, they may encounter issues or suggest improvements. It's important to listen to this feedback and make changes to the mechanics as needed. This can involve adjusting values, adding or removing features, or reworking entire systems. It's also important to keep in mind that gameplay mechanics should be fun, intuitive, and balanced in order to create a more enjoyable game experience for players.

In addition to playtesting and iterating, it's also important to consider the technical aspects of gameplay mechanics. This can involve programming and debugging, as well as performance optimization in order to ensure that the mechanics run smoothly on different devices and platforms. Properly implementing and optimizing gameplay mechanics requires a strong foundation in programming and technical skills, as well as an understanding of the hardware and software limitations of the target platform.

It's important to test gameplay mechanics on a variety of devices and platforms in order to ensure that they work as intended and perform well. This can involve testing on different hardware configurations, as well as simulating different network conditions to ensure that the mechanics work well in a range of situations.

As a solo game developer, building and refining gameplay mechanics can be a challenging but rewarding task. It requires a strong understanding of game design principles, as well as the ability to iterate and test your ideas effectively. Here are some key considerations for building and refining gameplay mechanics as a solo game developer:

- **Start with a clear vision**: Before you start building gameplay mechanics, it's important to have a clear vision of what you want to achieve. This includes defining the core gameplay mechanics, the core loop, and the overall feel of the game. You should also consider the target audience and the platforms you want to release on.

- **Use prototyping to test your ideas**: Prototyping is a crucial part of game development, and it's especially important for solo developers. Prototyping allows you to test and validate your ideas quickly and cheaply, and it can help you identify and fix problems early on. There are many different approaches to prototyping, including paper prototyping, digital prototyping, and hybrid prototyping. Choose the approach that best fits your needs and resources.

- **Playtest and gather feedback**: Playtesting is an essential part of game development, and it's especially important for solo developers who don't have a team to rely on. Playtesting allows you to gather valuable feedback from players and identify issues or problems that you might have missed. You can playtest your game with friends, family, or other trusted testers, and you can use tools like Google Forms or Trello to gather and organize feedback.

- **Iterate and refine**: Game development is an iterative process, and it's important to be open to change and willing to make adjustments as needed. As you playtest and gather feedback, you may discover that certain mechanics need to be adjusted, or that you need to add or remove features. Be prepared to iterate and refine your gameplay mechanics until they are fun, intuitive, and balanced.

In addition to technical considerations, it's also important to consider the balance of gameplay mechanics. This refers to the way in which different mechanics and systems interact with each other and affect the overall gameplay experience. For example, if a certain gameplay mechanic is too powerful or too easy to use, it can unbalance the game and make it less enjoyable for players. On the other hand, if a mechanic is too difficult or too weak, it can also create frustration for players.

Balancing gameplay mechanics can be a complex and iterative process, and it often requires extensive playtesting and feedback from players. It may involve adjusting values and parameters, as well as adding or removing features in order to achieve the desired balance.

In summary, building and refining gameplay mechanics is a crucial part of the production phase of game development, and it requires a combination of creative and technical skills. By prototyping and playtesting your mechanics, and considering the technical and balance aspects of gameplay, you can create a more enjoyable and engaging game experience for your players.

Creating levels and environments

Creating levels and environments is an important part of game development, as it helps to set the stage for gameplay and establish the world in which the game takes place. In this chapter, we'll be discussing some key considerations and techniques for creating levels and environments for your game.

One of the first things to consider when creating levels and environments is the overall theme and aesthetic of your game. This will help to set the tone and mood, and it will also help to define the visual style of your levels and environments. Some common themes and aesthetics for games include fantasy, science fiction, horror, and historical settings, but the possibilities are endless. It's important to choose a theme and aesthetic that fits your game concept and resonates with your target audience.

Once you've chosen a theme and aesthetic, you'll need to start designing and building your levels and environments. This can involve sketching out rough layouts and concepts or creating more detailed 3D models and assets. There are many different software tools and techniques that you can use to create levels and environments, depending on your skills and resources. Some popular tools for level design include 3D modelling software, level editors, and game engines.

In addition to creating the visual aspects of your levels and environments, you'll also need to consider the gameplay mechanics and challenges that will be included in each level. This can involve designing puzzles, obstacles, enemies, and other gameplay elements, and placing them throughout the level in a way that is balanced and challenging for the player. It's important to playtest your levels and environments as you build them, in order to identify and fix any issues or balance problems.

Another key aspect of creating levels and environments is lighting and atmosphere. Lighting can have a big impact on the mood and atmosphere of a level or environment, and it can also affect gameplay in various ways. For example, lighting can be used to create tension, guide the player's attention, or reveal hidden details. There are many different techniques for lighting levels and environments, and it's important to choose the right approach for your game.

There are several steps to creating levels and environments for your game:

- **Plan and design the layout**: Start by sketching out the layout of your level on paper or in a digital tool. Consider the size, shape, and flow of the space, as well as the placement of key elements such as platforms, obstacles, enemies, and collectibles. Think about how the layout will challenge and engage the player, and how it will support the gameplay mechanics and goals of the game.

- **Build the level**: Once you have a clear idea of the layout, start building the level in your game engine or level editor. Use prefabricated assets or create custom assets as needed to fill the space and bring your design to life. Pay attention to the details, such as lighting, texturing, and decoration, as they can greatly enhance the look and feel of the level.

- **Test and iterate**: Playtest your level as you build it and gather feedback from other players. This will help you identify and fix any issues or problems and improve the overall quality and enjoyment of the level. Don't be afraid to make changes and try out new ideas as you go.

- **Repeat**: Repeat the process for each level or environment in your game. Consider how the levels fit together, and how they contribute to the overall progression and narrative of the game.

Creating levels and environments can be a challenging and time-consuming task, but it can also be very rewarding. By putting in the effort to create well-designed and visually appealing spaces, you can greatly enhance the player experience and make your game more memorable and enjoyable.

Finally, it's important to consider the performance and optimization of your levels and environments. This can involve optimizing the use of graphics, memory, and other resources, in order to ensure that your game runs smoothly and efficiently on different devices and platforms. There are several tools and techniques that you can use to optimize your levels and environments, such as reducing the number of polygon faces, using texture compression, and using level of detail (LOD) systems. It's also important to test your levels and environments on different devices and platforms, and to make any necessary adjustments based on your findings. Optimization can be a time-consuming and complex process, but it's essential for creating a smooth and enjoyable player experience.

Creating levels and environments is one of the most important parts of game development, as it helps to set the stage for the gameplay and storytelling in your game. It requires a combination of artistic and technical skills, as you must not only create visually appealing environments, but also ensure that they are functional and optimized for gameplay.

When designing levels and environments, it's important to consider the theme, mood, gameplay, and performance. You'll want to create immersive and engaging spaces that reflect the overall tone of your game, and that provide a challenging and enjoyable experience for your players. As you work on your levels and environments, be sure to gather feedback and iterate on your designs to ensure that they are as polished and effective as possible. By putting time and effort into your levels and environments, you can create a rich and memorable player experience that will keep your players coming back for more.

Implementing art and audio

Implementing art and audio is a crucial part of game development, as it helps to bring your game to life and create an immersive player experience. Not only do these elements contribute to the overall aesthetic and atmosphere of your game, but they also play a crucial role in conveying information, emotions, and gameplay mechanics to the player.

There are several ways to approach implementing art and audio into your game. One option is to create all of the art and audio assets yourself. This can be a time-consuming process, but it allows you to have complete control over the look and feel of your game. If you have the skills and resources to create your own art and audio, it can be a rewarding and satisfying experience. Whether you're creating your own art and audio or working with a team, it's important to consider the style, quality, and performance of your assets, and to ensure that they support and enhance the overall vision of your game.

As a solo game developer, you'll need to be especially resourceful and efficient when it comes to implementing art and audio. You'll need to choose the right tools and techniques for creating and integrating your assets, and you'll need to manage your time and resources carefully.

Alternatively, you can source art and audio assets from external sources. This can include purchasing assets from asset stores or hiring freelancers to create custom assets for you. Sourcing assets externally can save you time and effort, but it's important to make sure you are using high-quality assets that fit the style and theme of your game. It's also important to properly license and credit any external assets you use.

Regardless of whether you create the assets yourself or source them externally, it's important to plan out the art and audio needs of your game in advance. This can help you determine the scope and budget of your project, and it can also help you ensure that you have all the assets you need when you need them.

Once you have your art and audio assets, the next step is to implement them into your game. This can involve using game development software or tools to integrate the assets into your game, as well as adjusting settings and parameters to get the desired effect. It's important to pay attention to detail and to test your art and audio assets to make sure they are working as intended.

In addition to implementing art and audio assets, it's also important to consider the overall performance and optimization of your game. This can involve minimizing the use of graphics and audio assets to reduce strain on the hardware, as well as optimizing the loading and streaming of assets to improve the overall player experience.

Here are some tips and considerations to help you get started:

- **Choose the right tools and software**: There are many tools and software options available for creating and integrating art and audio in your game. Some popular tools include 3D modelling software, 2D art software, audio editors, and game engines.

Research and evaluate different options, and choose the tools that best fit your needs and budget.

- **Create a style guide**: A style guide is a document that outlines the visual and audio aesthetic of your game. It can include things like colour schemes, character designs, music and sound effects, and other details. A style guide helps to ensure consistency and coherence in your art and audio, and it can be a useful reference for you or your team.

- **Create a workflow and pipeline**: A workflow is a set of steps that you follow to create and integrate your art and audio assets. A pipeline is a system for managing and organizing your assets as they move through your workflow. A well-defined workflow and pipeline can help you to stay organized, efficient, and productive, and it can prevent delays and errors.

- **Create and optimize your assets**: When creating your art and audio assets, it's important to consider their quality, performance, and size. High-quality assets can make a big difference in the look and feel of your game, but they can also consume more resources and take longer to create. Optimizing your assets can help you to balance quality and performance, and it can improve the overall performance of your game. Optimization can involve techniques such as reducing the number of polygons in 3D models, using compressed audio formats, or using sprite sheets for 2D graphics. It's important to test your assets in different devices and settings to ensure that they are performant and look good across a range of hardware.

In addition to creating and optimizing your assets, it's also important to manage them effectively. This can involve organizing your assets in a logical and consistent way, using version control or asset management tools to track changes, and backing up your assets regularly. By managing your assets effectively, you can save time and reduce the risk of errors or lost work.

Finally, it's important to consider the legal and ethical aspects of using art and audio assets in your game. This can involve obtaining permission to use assets created by others or crediting the creators of assets you use. It's also important to respect the copyright and intellectual property rights of others, and to avoid using assets that are protected by these rights without permission. By adhering to legal and ethical standards, you can avoid legal issues and build a positive reputation as a game developer.

Implementing art and audio is a pivotal part of game development, as it helps to bring your game to life and create an immersive player experience. It involves creating and optimizing art and audio assets and integrating them into your game using specialized tools and techniques.

When creating your art and audio assets, it's important to consider their quality, performance, and size. High-quality assets can make a big difference in the look and feel of your game, but they can also consume more resources and take longer to create. Optimizing your assets can help you to balance quality and performance, and it can improve the overall performance of your game.

In addition to creating and optimizing your assets, it's also important to consider the technical aspects of art and audio integration, such as file formats, resolution, and compatibility. By mastering the art and audio integration process, you can create a visually and sonically stunning game that will engage and delight your players.

Managing your time and resources

As a solo game developer, managing your time and resources well is pivotal for the success of your project. Effective time management is a key skill for any solo game developer, and it requires discipline, organization, and planning. Time is a limited and valuable resource, and it's important to use it wisely and efficiently. One way to do this is to set clear goals and priorities for your project, and to break them down into smaller, more manageable chunks. This can help you to focus on what's most important, and to avoid getting overwhelmed or side-tracked.

It's also important to create a schedule or plan for your project, and to stick to it as much as possible. This can involve setting aside specific times of the day or week for different tasks, and it can help you to stay on track and make progress. However, it's important to be flexible and adaptable, as game development can be unpredictable, and things may not always go according to plan.

In addition to creating a schedule, it can be helpful to set specific goals or milestones for your project, and to track your progress towards achieving them. This can help you to stay motivated and focused, and to see the progress you are making. It can also be helpful to set aside dedicated time for different tasks, such as programming, art, design, or audio. By focusing on one task at a time, you can increase your productivity and avoid multitasking, which can be stressful and inefficient.

In addition to managing your time, it's also important to manage your resources effectively. This can involve budgeting your money and other resources, such as assets, tools, and software. It's important to be aware of your limitations and to make smart, cost-effective decisions.

Effective resource management is also important for solo game developers, as it can help you to optimize your time and budget. This may involve budgeting your money and other resources, such as assets, tools, and software. It's important to be aware of your limitations and to make smart, cost-effective decisions. One way to optimize your resources is to reuse or recycle assets wherever possible, and to find ways to cut costs or save time. This can involve using free or low-cost tools and software or finding ways to automate or streamline your workflow. It can also involve seeking help or support from others, such as collaborators, mentors, or online communities.

Effective time management is not just about maximizing the time you spend working on your game. It also involves taking breaks and avoiding burnout. Working long hours without rest can lead to physical and mental fatigue, which can negatively impact your productivity, creativity, and overall well-being. It's important to have a good work-life balance, and to take time to rest and recharge. This can involve taking regular breaks throughout the day, as well as setting aside time for leisure and relaxation. It can also involve finding ways to reduce stress and manage your workload, such as delegating tasks or seeking help from others.

Taking care of your physical and mental health is crucial for the success of your project, and it's important to make it a priority. By finding the right balance between work and rest, you can maintain your energy, focus, and motivation, and increase your chances of creating a great game. This can involve eating well, getting enough sleep, and engaging in regular exercise and other activities that promote well-being. It can also involve seeking help if you are struggling with stress, anxiety, or other mental health issues that may be affecting your ability to work effectively.

Remember, it's OK to seek support and help when needed, whether it's through therapy, meditation, or simply talking to friends or loved ones. By taking care of yourself, you can maintain your energy and focus, and be more productive and successful in your work.

Effective resource management also involves making use of tools and techniques that can help you to stay organized and on track. This can include using project management software or apps to create to-do lists, schedule tasks, and track your progress. It can also involve using productivity techniques such as the Pomodoro Technique, which involves working for set periods of time followed by short breaks, or the 80/20 rule, which suggests that focusing on the most important tasks can lead to the greatest results.

In addition, it's important to stay up to date with new tools, techniques, and best practices in game development, as this can help you to improve your efficiency and effectiveness. This can involve joining online communities, attending workshops or conferences, or seeking out mentors or advisors who can provide guidance and support.

Effective time management also involves setting boundaries and knowing when to say no. It can be tempting to take on every opportunity or task that comes your way, but it's important to be realistic about what you can handle, and to prioritize your time and energy accordingly. This may involve delegating tasks to others, or simply saying no to requests that are not aligned with your goals or values.

In summary, managing your time and resources effectively as a solo game developer is crucial for the success of your project. It involves setting clear goals and priorities, creating a schedule or plan, optimizing your resources, maintaining a good work-life balance, taking care of your physical and mental health, and building relationships and networks. By being proactive and efficient, you can make the most of your time and resources and increase your chances of creating a great game.

Debugging and fixing issues

No matter how well you plan and test your game, it's almost certain that you'll encounter bugs and other issues at some point. These issues can range from small, cosmetic problems to major game-breaking issues, and they can be frustrating and time-consuming to fix. Debugging and fixing issues is an important part of the game development process, and it requires patience, persistence, and problem-solving skills. When you encounter an issue, it's important to try to reproduce it, in order to understand the circumstances and conditions under which it occurs. This can help you to narrow down the cause of the issue, and to come up with a plan to fix it.

There are many different tools and techniques that you can use to help you debug and fix issues. These can include debuggers, profilers, log files, and other tools that can help you to trace the cause of the issue and identify potential solutions. It's also important to have a good understanding of how your game works, and to be familiar with the code, assets, and systems that are involved. This can help you to identify patterns, trends, and potential sources of problems.

In addition to using tools and techniques, it's also important to have a systematic and methodical approach to debugging and fixing issues. This can involve creating a list of steps or a flowchart to follow, in order to help you to systematically test and eliminate potential causes of the issue. It can also involve working with other developers or users, in order to gather more information and get additional perspectives on the issue.

Next, gather as much information as you can about the problem. This can include error messages, logs, screenshots, and other relevant data. The more you know about the problem, the easier it will be to find a solution.

Once you have a good understanding of the problem, it's time to start debugging and fixing it. This can involve using tools such as debuggers, profilers, and testing frameworks, or it can involve manual testing and trial-and-error. It's important to be patient and persistent, and to keep an open mind. Sometimes, the solution to a problem can be counterintuitive or unexpected.

In addition to debugging and fixing issues, it's also important to prevent issues from occurring in the first place. One way to do this is to use testing and QA (quality assurance) techniques, such as unit testing, integration testing, and regression testing, to identify and fix problems before they reach the player. It's also important to use version control and other software development practices, such as code reviews, to ensure that your code is of high quality and easy to maintain.

Another way to prevent issues is to test your game thoroughly throughout the development process. This can involve using automated testing tools, as well as manual testing and playtesting. By catching and fixing issues early on, you can save time and effort in the long run.

There are many debugging tools available for game development, and the specific tools that you use will depend on the programming language, platform, and engine that you are using. Here are a few commonly used debugging tools:

- **Print statements**: One of the simplest and most basic debugging tools is the use of print statements. By adding print statements to your code, you can print out the values of variables or messages at various points in your code. This can help you to track down where an error is occurring or what the value of a variable is at a given point.

- **Debuggers**: A debugger is a tool that allows you to step through your code line by line, examining the values of variables and the state of the program at each step. This can help you to identify where an error is occurring and how to fix it.

- **Logging**: Logging involves recording messages or events to a log file, which can be helpful for tracking down issues that occur during runtime.

- **Profilers**: A profiler is a tool that allows you to analyse the performance of your code, including how long each function or section of code takes to execute. This can help you to identify areas of your code that are causing performance issues.

- **Memory analysers**: A memory analyser is a tool that allows you to analyse the memory usage of your program. This can be helpful for identifying memory leaks or other issues that can cause performance problems.

- **Testing frameworks**: Testing frameworks are tools that allow you to automate the testing of your code, including running tests and checking for errors. This can help you to catch issues early on and ensure that your code is working as expected.

Finally, it's important to be persistent and resilient when debugging and fixing issues. Game development can be challenging, and there will be times when you encounter roadblocks or setbacks. It's important to stay positive and focused, and to keep trying different approaches until you find a solution. By being proactive and persistent, you can overcome any challenges that come your way and create a great game.

Conclusion

Producing a videogame as a solo developer requires a hugely diverse set of skills and abilities. The task ahead can seem overwhelming for anyone just getting started on their game development journey. But with a strong foundation in various technical and artistic disciplines, such as programming, art, audio, and design, and the ability to work effectively as part of a team, communicate clearly and effectively, and manage your time and resources effectively, you'll be well equipped to handle the challenges of game production. It's also important to be adaptable and able to handle setbacks and challenges, and to stay motivated and focused throughout the development process.

In order to be successful in the production phase, it's important to have a strong foundation in various technical and artistic disciplines, such as programming, art, audio, and design. You'll also need to be able to work effectively as part of a team, communicate clearly and effectively, and manage your time and resources efficiently. It's also important to be able to adapt to change, handle setbacks and challenges, and stay motivated and focused throughout the development process.

Building and refining gameplay mechanics is a crucial part of the production phase, and it involves deciding on the mechanics, implementing and testing them, and iterating based on player feedback. It's important to ensure that the mechanics are fun, intuitive, and balanced, and one way to do this is through prototyping and playtesting.

Creating levels and environments is another important aspect of game development, and it involves building immersive and engaging environments that support the gameplay and theme of the game. It's important to consider the theme, mood, gameplay, and performance of your levels and environments, and to iterate and refine them based on feedback and testing.

Implementing art and audio involves creating and optimizing assets and integrating them into the game. This can involve creating and editing art and audio assets, as well as implementing them in the game engine. It's important to consider the quality, performance, and size of your assets, and to optimize them in order to balance quality and performance.

Managing your time and resources effectively is crucial for the success of your project. It involves setting clear goals and priorities, creating a schedule or plan, and optimizing your resources in order to make the most of your time and resources. It's also important to have a good work-life balance, and to take breaks in order to avoid burnout.

Finally, debugging, and fixing issues is an important part of game development, and it involves troubleshooting and fixing problems that arise in the game. This can involve debugging code, testing and fixing gameplay mechanics, and fixing art and audio issues. It's important to be proactive and efficient when debugging and fixing issues, to minimize delays and ensure that the game is stable and enjoyable for players.

As a solo game developer, it can be difficult to tackle every aspect of development on your own. This is where outsourcing can come in handy. Outsourcing refers to hiring external individuals or companies to handle specific tasks or responsibilities for your game. This can help you to save time, resources, and energy, and it can allow you to focus on the tasks that are most important to you.

However, it's important to carefully consider the tasks that you outsource, and to choose the right people or companies to work with. You'll want to ensure that they have the necessary skills and experience, and that they are reliable and trustworthy. It's also important to communicate clearly and effectively with your outsourced team members, in order to ensure that the work is completed to your satisfaction. By outsourcing tasks effectively, you can enhance the quality and scope of your game and increase your chances of success.

In conclusion, chapter 3: Production is really just the result from all your planning in Chapter 2, but it involves a wide range of tasks and skills. By mastering these tasks and skills, you can create a great game that stands the test of time.

Chapter 4:
Marketing and Distribution

Introduction

As a solo game developer, marketing and distributing your game can be a daunting and challenging task. However, it is also an incredibly important part of the game development process, and it can make a big difference in the success of your game.

Marketing is all about getting the word out about your game and attracting players. It involves promoting your game through various channels, such as social media, forums, and website marketing. Marketing and distributing your game is essential for getting it in front of potential players, and for building buzz and excitement around your game. Without a solid marketing and distribution plan, it can be difficult to reach a wide audience and to generate the sales and revenue that you need to sustain your game development efforts.

Distribution refers to the process of getting your game into the hands of players. This can involve selling your game through online marketplaces, such as Steam or the App Store, or through other distribution platforms. Distribution can also involve physical copies of your game, such as through retail stores or direct mail.

Marketing and distributing your game as a solo developer presents a unique set of challenges and opportunities. On the one hand, you don't have the resources or support of a large publisher or studio, which can make it harder to get your game noticed and to reach a wide audience. On the other hand, being a solo developer also gives you more control and flexibility, and it allows you to be nimble and responsive to changing market conditions and player feedback.

As a solo game developer, you may face some unique challenges and opportunities when it comes to marketing and distributing your game. On the one hand, you have complete control over the marketing and distribution process, and you can tailor your strategy to fit your needs and goals. On the other hand, you may have limited resources and experience, and you may have to work harder to get noticed and reach a wider audience.

Despite these challenges, marketing and distributing your game solo can be a rewarding and fulfilling experience. By taking control of the marketing and distribution process, you can build a strong connection with your players and create a lasting impact with your game.

In the past, distributing a game often involved producing physical copies and distributing them through retail channels. This process could be costly, time-consuming, and logistically challenging, especially for small and independent developers. However, with the rise of digital distribution platforms, it is now much easier for game developers, including solo developers, to distribute their games digitally. Digital distribution platforms such as Steam, Epic Games Store, and GOG allow developers to sell and distribute their games directly to players, without the need for physical copies.

In addition, console manufacturers such as PlayStation, Xbox, and Nintendo have also embraced digital distribution, allowing developers to release their games on their respective online stores, as well mobile phone marketplaces, such as the App Store, and Google Play. This makes it easier than ever before for developers, especially solo developers, to reach a global audience and get their games into the hands of players. However, it is important to note that while digital distribution has made it easier to reach players, it has also led to an oversaturation of the market, making it more challenging for developers to stand out and be noticed.

In this chapter, we'll be exploring the importance of marketing and distribution in the game development process, and we'll be looking at the challenges and opportunities that you'll face as a solo game developer. We'll be covering topics such as building a marketing plan, getting press coverage, using social media and other channels to reach players, and navigating the various platforms and distribution channels that are available. Whether you're just starting out on your game development journey or you're an experienced developer, we hope that this chapter will provide you with the knowledge and skills that you need to successfully market and distribute your game.

Building a website and social media presence

As a solo game developer, building a website and social media presence is a key part of marketing and distributing your game. A website is a central hub for information about your game, and it can serve as a place for players to learn more about the game, download demos or trailers, and purchase the full game. A website can also be a valuable asset for your game, as it can help to establish your brand, build credibility, and establish trust with your players. Building a website for your game can involve choosing a domain name and hosting provider, designing and building the website, and populating it with content such as screenshots, videos, and descriptions of your game.

Setting up a website for your game can be a relatively straightforward process, and there are many tools and platforms available to help you get started. Some popular options for game developers include WordPress, Squarespace, and Wix. These platforms offer a range of templates and customization options, and they can help you to create a professional-looking website with minimal effort.

Once you have your website set up, it's important to start building a social media presence on platforms like Twitter, Facebook, and Instagram. Social media platforms can be powerful tools for promoting your game and engaging with players. These platforms allow you to share updates, gather feedback, and build a community around your game. You can use social media to share updates about your game, as well as behind-the-scenes content, media, and other content. You can also use social media to gather feedback from your players, and to engage with them in a more personal and interactive way.

Building a social media presence involves creating accounts on these platforms, and then posting regular updates, such as new screenshots, videos, and news about your game. It's important to be active and responsive on social media, and to use it to build relationships with your players.

Building a social media presence can be a time-consuming task, but it is also an incredibly valuable investment for your game. By using social media to share updates, gather feedback, and engage with your players, you can build a loyal and passionate community around your game. This can help to drive awareness, interest, and sales for your game, and it can be a key factor in its success.

Using social media effectively can involve crafting a voice and tone that is authentic and engaging, and that represents the personality of your game. It can also involve experimenting with different types of content, such as behind-the-scenes glimpses, polls, and Q&As. In addition, it's important to use hashtags and other tags to make your content discoverable, and to engage with other users and communities that are relevant to your game. By building a strong social media presence, you can reach a wider audience, generate buzz and interest, and build a community of loyal fans around your game.

Twitch and YouTube are both popular platforms that can be used for marketing and distributing your game. Twitch is primarily focused on live streaming, and it is a great platform for showcasing your game in action, interacting with viewers, and building a community. YouTube is a video sharing platform that can be used to share trailers, gameplay videos, and other content related to your game. Both platforms can be a powerful way to reach a wide audience, and they can be a great way to get your game noticed and generate buzz.

However, it is important to keep in mind that building a following on these platforms takes time and effort, and it requires consistency and engagement. It is also important to follow the guidelines and terms of service for each platform, and to be respectful of the community. By leveraging the power of Twitch and YouTube, you can create a strong online presence and reach a wider audience for your game.

Going viral refers to when a piece of content, such as a video, tweet, or meme, spreads rapidly and widely through the internet, often through social media platforms. This can be a powerful and effective way to promote your game, as it can lead to a sudden and dramatic increase in exposure and awareness. However, going viral is also difficult to predict and control, and it can be a somewhat random and unpredictable occurrence. There are no guarantees when it comes to going viral, but there are things you can do to increase your chances.

This can involve creating high-quality, unique, and shareable content, using hashtags and other techniques to increase visibility, and engaging with your audience and building a community around your game. Ultimately, going viral is just one aspect of marketing and promotion, and it should be part of a larger and more comprehensive strategy for promoting your game.

A devlog is a record of the development process of a game, typically shared with the public through a blog or vlog format. Sharing a devlog can be a valuable marketing tool for solo game developers, as it allows them to document their progress, share updates and behind-the-scenes content, and engage with their audience.

By regularly sharing devlogs, solo developers can build a sense of community and anticipation around their game and provide transparency into their development process. Devlogs can also be a useful source of feedback and support, as they allow players and other developers to follow along and provide input or assistance. Overall, sharing a devlog can be a powerful way for solo game developers to market their game and connect with their audience.

In summary, building a website and social media presence is an important part of marketing and distributing your game as a solo developer. A website can serve as a central hub for information about your game, and it can help you to establish credibility and professionalism.

Social media platforms like Twitter, Facebook, and Instagram can help you to share updates, gather feedback, and engage with players. By building a strong and active presence on these platforms, you can build a community of fans and supporters who are interested in your game and willing to help spread the word.

However, it's important to be mindful of your time and energy when using social media, and to find a balance that works for you. By being strategic and consistent in your use of social media, you can effectively market and distribute your game as a solo developer.

Gathering feedback and reviews

As a solo game developer, gathering feedback from players is an essential part of the marketing and distribution process. Feedback can help you to identify problems, bugs, and other issues that may not have been apparent during development, and it can provide valuable insights into what players like and dislike about your game. There are a variety of ways to gather feedback, including:

- **Playtesting**: Playtesting involves gathering a group of players to test your game and provide feedback. This can be done in-person, online, or through a playtesting service. Playtesting can help you to identify issues and bugs, as well as to gather ideas for improvements and new features.

- **Social media**: Social media platforms like Twitter, Facebook, and Instagram are great places to engage with players and gather feedback. You can use these platforms to share updates, ask for feedback, and answer questions from players. You can also use hashtags and join relevant groups and communities to reach a wider audience.

- **Forums and online communities**: There are many forums and online communities dedicated to game development, and these can be great places to gather feedback and engage with players. You can start a thread about your game, ask for feedback, and participate in discussions with other developers and players.

- **Beta testing**: Beta testing is a more structured form of playtesting, where players test an early version of your game in exchange for providing feedback. Beta testing can help you to identify and fix issues, as well as to gather valuable insights from players.

- **Surveys and questionnaires**: Surveys and questionnaires are a more formal way to gather feedback from players. You can use tools like Google Forms or SurveyMonkey to create and distribute surveys to players, and to gather data and insights.

In addition to gathering feedback, it's also important to encourage players to leave reviews and ratings for your game. Reviews and ratings can help to increase the visibility and credibility of your game, and they can also help to attract new players. To encourage players to leave reviews, you can ask for their feedback and include a link to the review page in your game or on your website. You can also offer incentives, such as in-game rewards or discounts, to players who leave reviews.

It's also important to be prepared for negative feedback, as it's inevitable that not everyone will enjoy your game. Dealing with negative feedback can be challenging, but it's important to remember that not everyone will have the same tastes and preferences, and it's an important part of the process. It's also important to listen to constructive criticism and use it to improve your game.

However Even if you don't agree with the feedback, it's important to remain respectful and keep a professional tone, and to avoid getting into personal or defensive arguments with players. It's important to listen to what players are saying, and to try to understand their perspective. You can use negative feedback as an opportunity to learn and improve, and to demonstrate to players that you value their input.

To summarise, gathering feedback and reviews is an essential part of the marketing and distribution process for solo game developers. It not only helps to improve the quality of your game, but it can also be a key factor in attracting new players and generating buzz. Playtesting is one way to gather feedback, as it allows you to get direct input from players and identify any issues or areas for improvement.

Encouraging players to leave reviews can also be helpful, as it gives you a sense of how well your game is being received, and it can provide valuable insights into what players like or dislike about your game. It's important to be proactive in encouraging reviews, as they can have a big impact on your game's visibility and reputation.

However, it's also important to be prepared for negative feedback, as it is inevitable that not everyone will enjoy your game. Dealing with negative feedback in a professional and respectful manner is crucial, as it can help to maintain your reputation and build trust with players. By gathering feedback and using it to improve your game, you can create a better player experience and increase the chances of success for your game.

Pricing and monetization strategies

For any solo game developer, pricing and monetization are important considerations for the success of your game. The price you set for your game will have a big impact on its success, and it's important to find a balance between making a profit and attracting players. There are several factors to consider when deciding on a price for your game, including the value you are providing to players, the competition, and your own costs and expenses.

Pricing and monetization strategies can vary greatly depending on the type of game you are creating and your target audience.

One way to monetize your game is through a one-time purchase model, where players pay a single price to access the game and purchase a copy of your game outright. This model can be simple and straightforward, and it can be a good option for games with high replay value or a large content offering, as it allows players to access everything upfront. However, it can also be a barrier to entry for some players, especially if your game is priced higher than similar games on the market.

Another option is to use in-app purchases, which allow players to buy additional content or features within the game. This can include things like new levels, characters, or items. This model can be a good way to monetize free-to-play games, and it can be a good option for games with a large player base or a strong retention rate, as it allows players to try the game for free and then purchase additional content as they progress. However, it's important to be careful with in-app purchases, as players can easily spend more money than they intended if the purchases are not well-balanced or transparent.

A third option is to use a subscription model, where players pay a regular fee to access the game. This can be a good option for games with ongoing updates or content, as it allows you to generate recurring revenue. However, it can also be a barrier to entry for some players, as they may not want to commit to a long-term subscription.

"Pay to win" is a term used to describe a monetization model where players can purchase in-game items or advantages that give them a significant advantage over other players. This can be a controversial model, as it can create an uneven playing field and discourage players from continuing to play the game. Some players may feel that they have to spend a lot of money in order to be competitive, which can lead to frustration and disappointment. On the other hand, "pay to win" models can be lucrative for game developers, as they can generate a lot of revenue through in-game purchases. It's important for solo game developers to consider the potential risks and benefits of a "pay to win" model when deciding on a monetization strategy for their game.

Loot boxes are virtual items that can be purchased in-game, often with real money, and they contain a random selection of other virtual items or in-game currency. They are a common monetization strategy in many games, especially free-to-play games, and they can be controversial because they can create a sense of uncertainty or pressure for players to spend more money to get the items they want. Some players may enjoy the thrill of the unknown and the possibility of getting a rare or valuable item, while others may view loot boxes as a form of gambling or exploitation. It's important for game developers to consider the potential consequences of implementing loot boxes, and to ensure that they are used in a fair and transparent manner.

Discounting your game at launch can be a useful way to attract more players and generate buzz. A lower price can make your game more appealing to players who may be on the fence about purchasing it, and it can help to differentiate your game from competitors. However, it's important to be aware that the first week and month of a game's release are often the busiest, and that sales tend to slow down after this initial period. As a result, it's important to be mindful of this when setting your price, as it can also affect your overall revenue and profitability, and to consider how you will maintain interest in your game over the long term.

After launch, you can also consider offering discounted rates during special sales periods, such as during the holiday season or on special occasions like Halloween or Valentine's Day. These sales can be a great way to attract new players and generate additional revenue, but it's important to consider how they may affect your overall pricing strategy and the perceived value of your game. It can be helpful to carefully plan out your discounts and sales in advance, and to track their impact on your revenue and player engagement.

In summary, pricing and monetization strategies are an important part of marketing and distributing your game as a solo developer. It's important to consider the value you are providing to players, the competition, and your own costs and expenses when deciding on a price for your game. Different monetization models, including one-time purchases, in-app purchases, and subscriptions, can all be effective ways to monetize your game, depending on the nature and scope of your game. It's important to avoid using 'pay to win' or 'loot box' models, as these can be controversial and potentially damaging to your game's reputation. By carefully considering your pricing and monetization strategies, you can maximize your revenue and profitability, while also providing a fair and enjoyable experience for your players.

Distributing your game on different platforms

Distributing your game on different platforms is an important part of the marketing and distribution process for solo game developers. There are many platforms available for you to choose from, each with their own unique features and benefits.

One popular platform for distributing games is Steam, which is a digital distribution platform developed by Valve Corporation. Steam is available for PC, Mac, and Linux, and it offers a variety of features for developers, including the ability to sell games, add in-game items and microtransactions, and collect player data.

Another platform to consider is the App Store, which is a digital distribution platform for iOS apps, including games. The App Store is available on iPhone, iPad, and iPod Touch, and it offers a variety of features for developers, including the ability to sell apps, offer in-app purchases, and collect player data.

Google Play is another platform to consider, which is a digital distribution platform for Android apps, including games. Google Play is available on Android phones and tablets, and it offers a variety of features for developers, including the ability to sell apps, offer in-app purchases, and collect player data.

In addition to these platforms, there are many other options available for distributing your game, such as the Microsoft Store, the Epic Games Store, and others. Each platform has its own unique features and benefits, and it's important to consider which one is the best fit for your game.

When distributing your game on different platforms, it's important to consider the requirements and policies of each platform, as well as the demographics and preferences of their users. It's also important to optimize your game for each platform, in order to ensure the best possible player experience. By carefully considering these factors, you can maximize your chances of success and reach a wide audience with your game.

As a solo game developer, it is important to consider how you will distribute your game on different platforms in order to maximize its visibility and discoverability. There are several platforms available for distributing your game, including Steam, the App Store, Google Play, and others. Each platform has its own unique features and requirements, and it is important to research and understand these in order to make the most of your distribution strategy.

One tip for optimizing your game's visibility and discoverability is to have a strong and consistent branding presence across all platforms. This can include using a cohesive logo, colour scheme, and marketing materials that reflect the theme and style of your game. It is also important to have a clear and compelling elevator pitch or marketing message that explains what makes your game unique and interesting to players.

Another tip is to use keywords and tags that are relevant to your game and that will help players to find it through search engines and recommendation algorithms. It is also helpful to use screenshots, videos, and other media that showcase the gameplay and features of your game in an appealing and informative way.

In addition to these tips, it is important to be active and engaged on social media and other online communities related to your game. This can involve sharing updates, engaging with players, and participating in relevant events and forums. By building a strong online presence, you can create a community of fans and supporters who can help to spread the word about your game and increase its visibility and discoverability.

In summary, optimizing your game's visibility and discoverability on different platforms is an important part of the marketing and distribution process for solo game developers. By having a strong branding presence, using relevant keywords and tags, showcasing your game through media, and building an online presence, you can increase the chances of success for your game.

It's also vitally important to take advantage of every opportunity to promote your game and get it in front of potential players. One way to do this is by distributing your game on multiple platforms, including Steam, App Store, Google Play, and others. Each platform has its own set of rules and requirements, and it's important to familiarize yourself with these before submitting your game.

In addition to distributing your game on different platforms, it's also important to optimize your game's visibility and discoverability. This can involve using relevant keywords and tags, optimizing your game's title and description, and using eye-catching graphics and videos to showcase your game. It can also involve utilizing features such as Early Access or demos, which can help to generate buzz and get players interested in your game.

Another strategy for promoting your game is by sharing updates and information on other websites and forums. This can involve creating a website or blog for your game and sharing updates and news on social media platforms such as Twitter, Facebook, and Instagram. It can also involve participating in online communities and forums related to your game's genre or theme and engaging with other developers and players.

Overall, distributing your game on different platforms and promoting it on other websites and forums is a crucial part of the marketing and distribution process for solo game developers. By taking advantage of these opportunities, you can increase the visibility and discoverability of your game and get it in front of a wider audience.

Conclusion

In conclusion, marketing and distribution are essential components of the game development process, and they can make a significant impact on the success of your game. In this chapter, we covered a range of topics related to marketing and distributing your game as a solo developer.

We discussed the importance of building a website and social media presence, as well as strategies for gathering feedback and reviews from players. We also covered pricing and monetization strategies, including different models and techniques for maximizing revenue and profitability.

Finally, we explored the various platforms you can use to distribute your game, and tips for optimizing visibility and discoverability on those platforms.

Marketing and distribution can be a challenging and time-consuming task for solo game developers, but it is also an incredibly rewarding one. By effectively marketing and distributing your game, you can reach a wider audience, create a better player experience, and increase the chances of success for your game.

Ultimately, the key to marketing and distributing your game is to be proactive, creative, and persistent, and to keep learning and adapting to new developments in the industry. By doing so, you can create a great game that appears on the radar of the right demographic, and sells well enough to turn a profit, and make the entire process worthwhile.

However, it's important to remember that there is no magic bullet to profitability, and it's a matter of testing and iterating to find the right approach for your game and your players. By staying up to date with trends and best practices in the industry, and by being proactive and strategic in your marketing and distribution efforts, you can increase your chances of success as a solo game developer.

Chapter 5:
Legal and Financial Considerations

Introduction

As a solo game developer, it's essential to not only focus on creating an engaging and entertaining game, but also to carefully consider the legal and financial aspects of your project. These considerations can seem intimidating and overwhelming, especially for those just starting out in the industry. However, by taking the time to understand and properly address these issues, you can protect your interests, minimize risk, and set yourself up for long-term success and sustainability in the business of game development.

Ignoring or failing to properly address legal and financial issues can have serious consequences, such as financial loss, legal disputes, and damage to your reputation. It is therefore essential to invest the time and effort into understanding and addressing these issues, even if it may seem overwhelming or tedious.

In this chapter, we will delve into a variety of legal and financial topics that are relevant to solo game developers. These include establishing a business structure, safeguarding your intellectual property, negotiating contracts, managing finances and budgeting, and more. It is essential to be aware of these topics and take the necessary steps to protect yourself and your business.

Additionally, it is always a good idea to seek the advice of qualified professionals, such as lawyers and financial advisors, when making significant decisions that could impact your business. By seeking guidance from experts, you can make informed and confident decisions that will benefit your game development venture.

While it's not possible to cover every legal and financial issue that may arise in game development, this chapter aims to provide a solid foundation of knowledge and understanding that will help you navigate these complex areas with confidence. By taking the time to understand and properly address these issues, you can focus on creating a great game, knowing that you have the necessary legal and financial protections in place.

Protecting your intellectual property

Protecting your intellectual property is an important legal and financial consideration. Your intellectual property (IP) refers to the creative and original ideas, expressions, and inventions that you create and develop as part of your game. This can include things like the game's code, design, art, music, and more.

It's essential to understand how to protect your own intellectual property (IP) as well as properly license and use the IP of others. Failing to do so can result in legal disputes and financial consequences that can seriously impact the success of your game.

When it comes to protecting your own IP, it's important to familiarize yourself with copyright, trademark, and patent law. Copyright law protects original works of authorship, such as artwork, music, and code. Trademark law protects branding elements, such as names, logos, and slogans, that distinguish your game from others. Patent law protects new and useful inventions or discoveries. By understanding these legal protections and taking steps to secure them, you can protect your IP and prevent others from using it without your permission.

There are several legal tools that can help you to protect your IP, including copyright, trademark, and patent law. It's important to understand the differences between these types of IP protection, and to determine which ones are appropriate for your game.

Copyright law protects the creative expression of an idea, such as the code, art, music, and other assets that make up your game. It gives you the exclusive right to use, reproduce, and distribute your game, and it allows you to prevent others from using your game without your permission. Copyright protection is automatically granted to you as soon as you create your game, but you can also register your game with the Copyright Office to get additional legal protections and remedies.

Trademark law protects words, symbols, or designs that identify and distinguish your game from others. In the context of game development, trademark law can protect things like your game's name, logo, and other branding elements. It allows you to prevent others from using your brand in a way that could confuse or mislead players. It's important to choose a unique and distinctive brand for your game, and to conduct a trademark search to ensure that your brand is available for use. You can then register your trademark with the Trademark Office to get additional legal protections and remedies.

It's also a good idea to use the ® symbol to indicate that your branding elements are registered trademarks, and to include a trademark notice in the credits of your game.

Patent law protects new and useful inventions, such as processes, machines, and products. In the context of game development, patent law can protect things like innovative gameplay mechanics or other unique features of your game. If you have developed a new game mechanic or other innovative feature for your game, you may be able to get a patent to protect it. However, patent law can be complex and expensive, and it may not be the best option for all game developers. It's important to seek the advice of a qualified patent attorney before deciding whether to pursue a patent.

It's important to note that IP protection is not automatic, and you must take steps to secure it. This can involve registering your IP with the appropriate government agency, such as the US Copyright Office or the US Patent and Trademark Office. It can also involve taking legal action to enforce your IP rights, if necessary.

It's also important to be aware of IP laws in other countries, as they can vary widely. If you plan to distribute your game internationally, it's a good idea to seek the advice of a qualified lawyer to ensure that you are complying with the relevant laws and protecting your IP appropriately.

In addition to protecting your own IP, it's also important to properly license and use the IP of others. This includes obtaining permission to use any third-party assets, such as music, artwork, or code, that you include in your game. Failing to do so can result in legal disputes and financial consequences, such as copyright infringement lawsuits or licensing fees. It's a good idea to use written contracts or licenses to clearly define the terms of use for any third-party IP, and to keep accurate records of your licensing agreements.

In summary, protecting your intellectual property and properly licensing and using the IP of others is an essential legal and financial consideration for solo game developers. By understanding copyright, trademark, and patent law, and taking steps to secure your IP, you can protect your creative ideas and innovations, and minimize the risk of legal disputes or financial consequences.

It's important to note that this chapter is just a brief overview of intellectual property law and how it applies to game development. There are many other resources available online that can provide more in-depth information on this topic.

However, it's always a good idea to seek the advice of a qualified lawyer or legal professional when making important decisions about your game's intellectual property. Protecting your intellectual property is a complex and nuanced process, and it's important to get it right in order to ensure the long-term success and sustainability of your business.

Don't take any chances with your game's intellectual property - seek professional advice and make sure that you have the necessary protections in place before releasing your game to the public.

Setting up a business or legal entity

One of the first legal and financial considerations you will need to address is setting up a business or legal entity. This is a hugely important step to consider in order to protect your interests and minimize risk. Setting up a separate business or legal entity can provide several benefits, including protecting your personal assets and making it easier to manage your finances. Choosing the right business structure is important, as it can have significant implications for your taxes, liability, and ability to raise capital.

There are several different business structures to choose from, including sole proprietorship, limited liability company (LLC), and corporation. Each has its own advantages and disadvantages, and the right choice for you will depend on your specific needs and circumstances.

A sole proprietorship is the simplest and most common business structure for solo game developers. A sole proprietorship is owned and operated by a single individual, and it doesn't have any formal requirements for formation. This structure is easy to set up and operate and requires minimal paperwork, and it offers complete control and flexibility to the owner. But it also offers the least protection for your personal assets.

In a sole proprietorship, you and your business are considered one and the same, meaning that their personal assets may be at risk if the business incurs any debts or liabilities or legal issues that may arise.

Another option is a limited liability company (LLC), which is a hybrid business structure that combines elements of a corporation and a sole proprietorship. A limited liability company (LLC) is a popular choice for solo game developers because it offers greater protection for your personal assets. An LLC offers the limited liability protection of a corporation, meaning that the owners' personal assets are generally not at risk if the business incurs any debts or liabilities.

In an LLC, the business is considered a separate entity from its owners, and the owners are not personally liable for any debts or legal issues that may arise. This can provide peace of mind, especially if you are concerned about potential lawsuits or other legal issues.

At the same time, an LLC is more flexible and easier to operate than a corporation, and it offers the ability to choose how it is taxed. However, it may be more expensive to set up and operate than a sole proprietorship, and it may have more formal requirements for formation and operation.

Finally, a corporation is a more formal and complex business structure that offers limited liability protection to its owners, similar to an LLC, and even greater protection for your personal assets. A corporation is a separate legal entity that is owned by shareholders, and it is managed by a board of directors and officers. This structure is more complex and expensive to set up and operate than a sole proprietorship or LLC, and it may have more formal requirements for formation and operation. Corporations are subject to more regulations and paperwork, and they may also be subject to higher taxes. However, it offers the ability to raise capital through the sale of stock, and it may be a good option for larger or more complex businesses.

Ultimately, the right business structure for you will depend on your specific needs and circumstances. It's a good idea to seek the advice of a qualified lawyer or financial professional to help you determine the best option for your situation.

When setting up your business, along with choosing the right business structure it's important to register your business and obtain any necessary licenses and permits. This may involve registering with your state or local government, and it may also involve obtaining specific licenses or permits. This can vary depending on your location and the type of business you are operating. It's a good idea to research the requirements in your area and make sure you have everything you need before you start operating your business. and obtaining the necessary documents is an important step to ensure that your business is legally compliant.

In addition to registering your business, it's also a good idea to set up a separate bank account for your business. This can help you to keep your personal and business finances separate, making it easier to track your income and expenses. It can also help to establish your business as a legitimate entity, which can be useful when seeking funding or working with clients or partners.

Maintaining accurate and organized financial records is also crucial for solo game developers. This can include keeping track of income and expenses, preparing financial statements, and creating a budget. There are several tools and software options available to help with record-keeping, such as QuickBooks or Excel. By staying on top of your finances, you can make informed decisions about your business and keep it running smoothly.

Other legal and financial considerations when setting up a business or legal entity include choosing a business name, obtaining any necessary licenses or permits, and obtaining insurance. These steps can help protect your interests and ensure that you are complying with all applicable laws and regulations.

It's important to note that setting up a business or legal entity is a complex process, and it's always a good idea to seek the advice of a qualified lawyer or financial professional before making any decisions. However, by taking the time to understand your options and set up your business correctly, you can protect your interests and set yourself up for success in the long term.

Creating contracts and agreements

It's important to have clear, legally binding contracts and agreements in place for any freelance work or collaborations that you engage in. Having a contract in place helps to protect both you and the other party, by clearly outlining the terms of the agreement and establishing a clear understanding of each party's responsibilities and expectations and helps to protect your interests and minimize risk.

It's valuable to have a thorough understanding of contracts and agreements in order to protect yourself and your business. This includes being able to draft contracts for freelance work or collaborations, negotiate terms and conditions with partners or investors, and use non-disclosure agreements (NDAs) to protect your confidential information.

When drafting or negotiating a contract, there are a few key things to consider. First, it's important to be clear and concise in your language. Ambiguity or unclear terms can lead to misunderstandings or disputes down the line.

Make sure to specify any important details, such as deadlines, deliverables, and payment terms.

It's also a good idea to include provisions for what will happen in the event of a breach of contract. This can include remedies such as fines or termination of the agreement.

Freelance work or collaborations can be a great way to bring new talent or expertise onto your project, but it's important to have a clear contract in place to protect both parties. There are a few key elements that should be included in any contract or agreement for freelance work or collaborations. These include the scope of the work, any deliverables or milestones, the payment terms and schedule, and any confidential or proprietary information that may be shared. It's also a good idea to include provisions for ownership of any intellectual property that is created, and for resolving any disputes that may arise.

Negotiating terms and conditions with partners or investors can be a complex process, and it's important to have a clear understanding of your own goals and priorities. It's also important to be aware of any potential legal or financial risks, and to seek the advice of a qualified lawyer or financial professional if necessary.

Some key points to consider when negotiating terms and conditions include:

- **Scope of work**: This should clearly describe the work that is being done, including any specific tasks or deliverables. Be clear about what tasks or responsibilities are included in the contract, and what is not. This will help to avoid misunderstandings or disputes down the line.
- **Compensation**: This should outline how the freelancer or collaborator will be paid, including the rate or fee, and any milestones or payment schedule. Make sure that the payment terms are clearly stated and fair. This may include a fixed fee, a percentage of profits, or some other arrangement.
- **Deadlines**: Set clear deadlines for the completion of tasks or milestones, and make sure that these are realistic and achievable.

- **Ownership**: This should specify who owns the rights to the work that is being produced, and any restrictions on use or distribution. If you are creating new intellectual property as part of the agreement, make sure that the ownership and licensing terms are clearly stated.
- **Confidentiality**: If the work involves confidential information or proprietary ideas, this should be addressed in the contract to protect both parties.
- **Termination**: This should outline the circumstances under which the contract can be terminated, and any provisions for terminating the agreement.

When drafting a contract or agreement, to be as specific and detailed as possible. This will help to avoid misunderstandings and conflicts down the line. It's also a good idea to have the contract reviewed by a lawyer or other legal professional to ensure that it is fair and legally enforceable. By having clear and legally binding contracts in place, you can protect your interests and avoid any misunderstandings or disputes.

Keep in mind that contracts are not one-size-fits-all. Different agreements will be appropriate for different situations. For example, a contract for freelance work will be different from a contract for a partnership or investment. Make sure to customize your contract to fit the specific needs of your situation.

When negotiating with partners or investors, it's important to be open and honest about your needs and expectations. Be willing to compromise, but don't be afraid to advocate for your own interests. It's a good idea to seek the advice of a lawyer or other legal professional to ensure that your contracts are fair and legally-binding. Be realistic about what you can offer and what you need in return. This may include equity in your company, a percentage of profits, or other forms of compensation. It's also essential to clearly outline the roles and responsibilities of each party, as well as any legal liabilities or obligations.

Non-disclosure agreements (NDAs) are another important tool for protecting your confidential information and intellectual property. An NDA is a legally binding agreement that requires one party to keep certain information confidential and not disclose it to anyone else. This can be useful in situations where you need to share sensitive information with partners or investors, or when working with freelance contractors.

It's important to remember that contracts and agreements are not just for protecting your interests, but also for building trust and good working relationships. By clearly outlining the terms and conditions of your collaborations, you can foster a positive and productive environment for creating great games together. Understanding how to draft, negotiate, and protect yourself with these tools, you can minimize risk and set yourself up for success in the business of game development.

Managing budgets and finances

As a solo game developer, managing budgets and finances is a crucial part of your business. It's important to have a clear understanding of your costs and expenses to make informed decisions about your project, and to ensure that you are able to complete your game within your financial means. It's essential to track your expenses and income in order to stay on top of your budget and ensure that your game is financially successful. This involves keeping accurate and organized records of all your financial transactions, including expenses for things like development costs, marketing, and legal fees, as well as income from sales, investments, and other sources.

It's vital to manage your budgets and finances effectively in order to ensure the success and sustainability of your project. One way to do this is by accurately estimating costs and setting budgets for game development. This can help you to avoid overspending and financial problems down the road.

One of the first steps in managing your budget is to estimate the costs associated with game development. This includes not only the cost of any external resources or services that you may need, such as art assets or marketing, but also the costs of your own time and efforts. It's a good idea to be as detailed as possible in your estimates, and to factor in contingencies for unexpected expenses or changes in scope.

Tracking expenses and income is also crucial for managing your budgets and finances. By keeping track of your spending and revenue, you can get a clear picture of your financial situation and make informed decisions about your project.

There are a number of ways you can track your expenses and income. One option is to use a spreadsheet program like Microsoft Excel or Google Sheets, as well as regularly reviewing your financial data. This allows you to create a budget template and input your financial data, which can then be easily organized and analysed. There are a variety of accounting software options available for solo game developers to choose from. Some popular options include QuickBooks, Xero, and

Wave. These programs can help you track your expenses, create invoices, and manage your overall financial situation. It's important to choose the right software that meets your specific needs and budget. Some factors to consider when selecting accounting software include the type of business you have, your financial management experience, and your budget. It may be helpful to research and compare different software options before making a decision. Additionally, it's always a good idea to consult with a financial professional to determine the best solution for your business.

Once you have a clear idea of your costs, you can set a budget for your game. This will help you to stay on track and make sure that you are using your resources wisely. It's also a good idea to establish a system for tracking your expenses, such as using a spreadsheet or budgeting software, so that you can see how your spending compares to your budget and make any necessary adjustments.

Regardless of the method you choose, it's important to regularly review and update your financial records in order to get a clear picture of your financial situation. This can help you to identify any areas where you may be overspending, and to make adjustments to your budget as needed. By staying on top of your finances, you can make informed decisions about how to allocate your resources and maximize your revenue.

There are many different funding options available to solo game developers, depending on your specific needs and goals. Some options include self-funding through personal savings or loans, crowdfunding platforms such as Kickstarter or Indiegogo, grants or awards from industry organizations, and investment from venture capital firms or angel investors. Each option has its own advantages and disadvantages, and it's important to carefully research and consider the best fit for your project.

Self-funding can provide more control and ownership but may not provide enough capital to fully realize your vision. Crowdfunding can be a great way to engage with and build a community around your game, but it also comes with risks and uncertainties. Grants and awards can provide financial support and recognition but may be competitive and have strict eligibility requirements.

Investment from outside sources can provide a significant influx of capital but may also come with strings attached and a loss of control. It's important to carefully weigh the pros and cons of each option and seek the advice of a financial professional before making a decision.

Working freelance while developing your game can be a good way to generate income and support yourself while working on your project. Freelancing allows you to take on short-term contracts or projects for other clients, which can provide a steady stream of income and help you build your skills and experience. It's important to manage your time effectively and make sure that you are able to balance your freelance work with your game development. It can also be helpful to set boundaries with clients and communicate your priorities and availability upfront to ensure that you are able to meet your deadlines and commitments.

Government funding is one option that solo game developers may consider when seeking financial support for their projects. This can include grants, loans, and other forms of financial assistance from federal, state, or local governments. Government funding programs may be available for specific types of projects, such as those that promote economic development, innovation, or social welfare.

Government funding for game development can vary significantly from one country to another. In some countries, there may be grants or tax breaks available specifically for game developers, while in others, these types of support may not exist. It's important for solo game developers to research the specific funding options available in their own country, and to explore all potential avenues for financial support. This may include looking into grants and tax breaks offered by national or local governments, as well as other funding sources such as crowdfunding platforms or private investors.

Keep in mind that the eligibility requirements and application processes for these types of funding can vary widely, and it may be necessary to put in significant time and effort in order to secure the necessary funding for your game project.

To be eligible for government funding, you may need to meet certain criteria, such as being a small business, having a certain level of revenue, or demonstrating a certain level of need. It's important to research the various government funding options available in your region and to carefully review the requirements and application processes for each one. It may also be helpful to seek the advice of a financial professional or grant writing specialist to increase your chances of success.

However, it's important to be cautious when seeking funding or investment. Make sure to do your research and carefully consider the terms and conditions of any agreements. It's always a good idea to seek the advice of a qualified financial professional or lawyer when making important financial decisions.

In addition to setting and tracking a budget, it's important to be mindful of your overall financial health as a business. This includes managing your cash flow, keeping track of your income and expenses, and making strategic financial decisions that will help to sustain your business in the long term. By being proactive and disciplined in your financial management, you can increase your chances of success as a solo game developer.

Conclusion

Managing budgets and finances is a crucial part of the game development process, particularly for solo developers, who may not have a team or investors to fall back on. It involves estimating costs, setting budgets, tracking expenses and income, and seeking funding or investment opportunities. Proper budgeting and financial management can help you ensure that you have the resources you need to complete your game, while also protecting your business and maximizing your profits.

There are various options for funding, including self-funding, working freelance, and seeking investment from partners or investors. Government grants and tax breaks may also be available in certain countries. It's important to carefully consider these options and choose the one that is most suitable for your project and business.

It's also critical to track your expenses and income, and to use accounting software to help manage your finances. This will allow you to stay organized and make informed decisions about your budget. By carefully managing your budgets and finances, you can ensure that you have the resources you need to complete your game and achieve your financial goals.

Some key points to keep in mind include:

- Estimating costs and setting a budget: This is essential for planning and organizing your game development process. By identifying all of your expenses and determining how much you can afford to spend, you can make informed decisions about how to allocate your resources.
- Tracking expenses and income: It's important to keep detailed records of your finances, including all income and expenses. This will help you to stay on top of your budget and make adjustments as needed.
- Seeking funding or investment opportunities: If you need additional resources to complete your game, there are various options available, including government grants, investor funding, and self-funding. Each option has its own pros

and cons, and it's important to carefully consider the best fit for your project.

- Working freelance while developing: If you're working on your game on the side while holding down another job or doing freelance work, it's important to keep your finances separate and track your income and expenses carefully. This will help you to stay organized and make the most of your time and resources.

Finally, it's always a good idea to seek the advice of a qualified financial professional when making important financial decisions. They can help you understand the legal and financial aspects of game development and provide guidance on the best course of action for your business. By following these tips and seeking expert advice, you can protect your interests and set yourself up for success in the world of game development.

In conclusion, the legal and financial considerations of game development are an essential part of the process for solo game developers. From protecting your intellectual property and setting up a business structure, to creating contracts and agreements and managing budgets and finances, these issues can seem complex and intimidating. However, by understanding these topics and taking the necessary steps, you can protect your interests, minimize risk, and set yourself up for long-term success and sustainability in the business of game development.

It's important to note that this chapter is not intended as financial advice, but rather as a guide to some of the options and considerations that solo game developers may encounter. As always, it's a good idea to seek the advice of a qualified lawyer or financial professional when making important decisions.

Chapter 6:
Staying Motivated and Managing Burnout

Introduction

As a solo game developer, you are likely to face many challenges and setbacks on your journey to creating a successful game. One of the biggest challenges you will likely face is staying motivated and avoiding burnout. Working on a game project can be a long and gruelling process, and it's easy to lose sight of your goals and become demotivated. Game development can be a rewarding and fulfilling pursuit, but it can also be stressful and demanding.

It's easy to get caught up in the excitement of creating a game and push yourself too hard, only to find that you are burnt out and unable to continue. Burnout is a state of physical, emotional, and mental exhaustion that can be caused by overwork or stress, and it can have a negative impact on your productivity and overall well-being.

In this chapter, we will explore strategies for staying motivated and managing burnout as a solo game developer. We will cover topics such as setting realistic goals, finding a healthy work-life balance, seeking support from others, and finding ways to stay energized and focused. We will also look at some common causes of burnout and ways to prevent it, as well as strategies for dealing with burnout if it does occur. By understanding and addressing these issues, you can avoid burnout and sustain your passion for game development over the long term.

It's important to note that everyone is different, and what works for one person may not work for another. It's important to find what works for you and to be proactive about managing your own well-being. With the right mindset and strategies, you can overcome the challenges of solo game development and achieve your goals.

Setting goals and priorities:

As a solo game developer, it's essential to set clear goals and priorities in order to stay motivated and on track. This is especially important when working on a long-term project like game development, which can be filled with challenges and setbacks. One effective way to set goals is to use the SMART criteria - Specific, Measurable, Attainable, Relevant, and Time-bound.

By setting goals that meet these criteria, you can create a roadmap for your game development journey and measure your progress along the way. When you have a clear roadmap and know what tasks and responsibilities are most important to your game development, it can help you stay focused and avoid getting overwhelmed.

For example, instead of setting a goal to "make a successful game," you could set a specific goal such as "release a game on Steam that generates $500 in revenue within 6 months." This goal is specific (it includes a target platform and revenue amount), measurable (you can track your progress towards the revenue goal), attainable (it's realistic to release a game on Steam and generate $500 in revenue within 6 months), relevant (releasing on Steam and generating revenue are important for your business), and time-bound (you have a clear deadline of 6 months).

Making your goals measurable allows you to track your progress and see how far you have come. Ensuring that your goals are attainable helps you stay realistic and avoid setting yourself up for disappointment. Making your goals relevant to your overall game development vision keeps you focused and motivated. And setting time-bound deadlines helps you stay on track and ensures that you are making progress towards your goals.

Identifying and prioritizing your tasks and responsibilities is also crucial for staying motivated and avoiding burnout. It's easy to get overwhelmed by all of the things you need to do, but by focusing on the tasks and responsibilities that are most important to your game development, you can ensure that you are making progress and staying on track. This might involve identifying the most critical features of your game or focusing on the tasks that will have the biggest impact on your progress.

In addition to setting specific goals, it's also helpful to create a roadmap for your game development journey. This can be a high-level plan that outlines the steps you need to take to achieve your goals, such as prototyping, designing, coding, testing, and marketing. By having a roadmap, you can stay focused on the tasks that will help you reach your goals and avoid distractions.

In addition to setting goals, it's also important to identify and prioritize the tasks and responsibilities that are most important to your game development. This can help you focus on what needs to be done and avoid getting side-tracked by less important tasks.

One way to do this is to use the 80/20 rule, also known as the Pareto principle. This principle states that roughly 80% of your results come from 20% of your efforts. By identifying the 20% of tasks and responsibilities that will have the biggest impact on your game development, you can focus on what matters most and make the most of your time and energy.

Another way to do this is by using the Eisenhower Matrix, which separates tasks into four categories: urgent and important, not urgent but important, urgent but not important, and neither urgent nor important. By focusing on the tasks in the urgent and important category, you can ensure that you are working on the most important tasks first and avoiding distractions.

To further break down large tasks into smaller, more manageable steps, you can use a tool such as the Pomodoro Technique. This involves setting a timer for a specific amount of time, usually 25 minutes, and focusing on a specific task until the timer goes off. Then, you take a short break before starting the next Pomodoro. By dividing your work into smaller chunks, you can stay focused and avoid feeling overwhelmed by large tasks.

It's also important to remember that game development is a marathon, not a sprint. It's easy to get caught up in the excitement of creating a new game and push yourself too hard, leading to burnout. That's why it's important to set realistic goals and pace yourself, taking breaks and time off when needed. By setting goals and priorities and managing your workload effectively, you can stay motivated and avoid burnout as you work towards completing your game.

Remember that you don't have to do everything yourself. Outsourcing or delegating tasks to others can be a great way to manage your workload and avoid burnout. By focusing on what you do best, and letting others handle the rest, you can create a more efficient and sustainable game development process.

It's also important to regularly review and adjust your goals and roadmap as needed. For example, if you realize that one of your goals is no longer relevant or attainable, you can revise it or set a new goal in its place. By regularly reviewing and adjusting your goals, you can stay motivated and on track.

Finally, it's essential to be mindful of your own mental and physical health. Taking regular breaks, getting enough sleep, and engaging in activities outside of game development can all help to prevent burnout and keep you motivated. By taking care of yourself, you'll be better able to handle the challenges of game development and stay focused on your goals.

Finding support and community

It can be easy to feel isolated and overwhelmed by the task ahead. This can make it difficult to stay motivated and avoid burnout, as you may not have anyone to turn to for support or guidance. The game development process is challenging and time-consuming, and it's natural to experience periods of doubt and frustration. That's why it's so important to seek out support and guidance from others in the industry. However, it's important to remember that you are not alone in this journey.

Having a supportive network can provide a sense of community, accountability, and camaraderie as you work on your game. It can also be a source of valuable feedback, advice, and resources as you navigate the challenges of game development.

There are many resources and communities available to support and guide you along the way. Here are a few suggestions:

- Join online forums or communities specifically for game developers. These can be great places to connect with others who are facing similar challenges, ask for advice, and share your own experiences. Some popular forums and communities include /r/gamedev on Reddit, the IGDA (International Game Developers Association) forum, and the Solo Game Developers subreddit.
- Attend game development conferences or meetups in your area. These events can be a great way to network with others in the industry, learn from professionals, and get inspired by new ideas.
- Consider working with a mentor or advisor. Having someone who has been through the game development process before and can offer guidance and support can be invaluable.
- Collaborate with other game developers. Working with others on a project can be a great way to share the workload, learn from each other, and stay motivated.

Discord is a communication platform that was originally designed for gamers, but has since been adopted by a wide range of communities. It allows users to communicate through text, voice, and video, and has features such as customizable servers, channels, and roles. Discord also has a range of integrations and tools that can be used to enhance the user experience, such as custom emojis and bots.

Many game developers use Discord as a way to connect with their community, share updates, and get feedback on their games. It can be a valuable resource for solo game developers who are looking for a supportive and engaged community.

Another way to build a supportive network is to seek out mentors or advisors who have experience in the game development industry. Seeking support and guidance from other game developers, mentors, or professionals can be incredibly beneficial for staying motivated and avoiding burnout. Not only can these individuals provide valuable advice and perspective, but they can also offer a sense of community and camaraderie. By connecting with others who are facing similar challenges, you can find motivation and support to keep going.

In addition to the support and guidance of others, it can also be helpful to surround yourself with a network of people who believe in your project and are supportive of your efforts. This might include friends, family, or even a dedicated group of supporters or fans. Having a strong support system can provide motivation and encouragement, and help you stay focused and motivated throughout the game development process. In addition to connecting with others, it's also helpful to seek out mentors or professionals who can offer guidance and support. This could be someone you know personally, or someone you admire from afar. Having someone to turn to for advice or a fresh perspective can be invaluable, especially when you're feeling stuck or overwhelmed.

Having support from family and friends outside of the game development industry can be incredibly valuable, especially during times of stress or uncertainty. These individuals can offer a different perspective, provide emotional support, and help to keep things in perspective. It's important to make time for these relationships and to communicate your needs and feelings with your loved ones. They may not always understand the specifics of game development, but they can still provide a listening ear and a comforting presence. Don't be afraid to seek support from these sources and to express your appreciation for their support.

It's natural to feel overwhelmed or stressed at times when working on a solo game development project, and having a strong network of supportive individuals can make a big difference. Whether it's through regular phone calls or video chats, scheduled hangouts, or simply sharing your thoughts and feelings, building and maintaining these relationships can provide a much-needed outlet and help you to feel less isolated. It's also important to remember that these relationships are a two-way street, and it's important to be there for your loved ones as well. So, take the time to cultivate and nurture these relationships, and you'll have a strong support system to turn to when things get tough.

It's important to have a life outside of game development, as it can help to prevent burnout and maintain a sense of balance and perspective. Taking breaks, pursuing hobbies and interests, and spending time with loved ones can all help to recharge your batteries and keep you motivated and engaged in your work. It's easy to get caught up in the hustle and grind of game development, especially as a solo developer, but it's essential to make time for other aspects of your life. Having a healthy work-life balance can also help to prevent burnout and maintain your overall well-being. Don't be afraid to take a step back from your work and prioritize your own needs and well-being.

Remember, **you don't have to go it alone**. Ultimately, finding support and community is a key factor of staying motivated and avoiding burnout as a solo game developer. By connecting with others and seeking out guidance and support, you can find the motivation and strength to keep going, even when the going gets tough.

Managing stress and burnout

It's essential to be aware of the signs of stress and burnout and to take proactive steps to manage them. Burnout can occur when you're working long hours, feeling overwhelmed, or not seeing progress in your work. It's important to recognize the signs of burnout, which can include feelings of exhaustion, cynicism, and ineffectiveness, as well as a loss of motivation or enjoyment in game development.

There may be physical symptoms too, such as headaches, trouble sleeping, and a decrease in productivity. If left unchecked, these feelings can lead to burnout, which can have serious consequences for your physical and mental health, as well as the quality and success of your game. **If you are experiencing these symptoms, it's important to take a step back** and assess what might be causing your stress.

To manage stress and prevent burnout, it's important to set boundaries and limits for yourself, both in terms of work and personal time and establish a healthy work-life balance. Make sure to take regular breaks and to set aside time for hobbies and activities that you enjoy outside of game development. It's also important to practice self-care, such as getting enough sleep, eating well, and exercising. Practice mindfulness and focus on the present moment. This can involve activities such as meditation, deep breathing, or journaling. These practices can help to clear your mind and allow you to approach your work with a fresh perspective.

There are many ways to prioritize self-care, and it's important to find what works best for you. Some ideas include:

- Exercise and physical activity: Exercise can help to reduce stress, improve your mood, and boost your energy levels. It's important to make time for physical activity, even if it's just a short walk or yoga session.
- Sleep: Getting enough rest is crucial for maintaining your physical and mental health. Make sure you're getting enough sleep each night and try to establish a consistent sleep routine.

- Nutrition: Eating well can help to boost your energy levels and improve your mood. It's important to make sure you're getting a balanced diet that includes plenty of fruits, vegetables, and other nutrients.
- Relaxation and mindfulness: Finding ways to relax and de-stress can help to manage your stress levels and prevent burnout. This could include activities such as meditation, yoga, or taking a hot bath.

It's also important to take breaks when you need them. This can be as simple as stepping away from your work for a few minutes to take a walk or do some stretching or taking a day or two off to rest and recharge. Remember, it's okay to take a break and come back to your work with fresh eyes and a clear mind.

Another effective way to manage stress and prevent burnout is to seek support from others, whether it's through a support group, therapy, or simply talking to friends and family. It's also important to communicate with your loved ones about your workload and to ask for help when you need it. Sharing your struggles and seeking guidance from those who have experienced similar challenges can be extremely beneficial. You might also consider seeking professional help, such as therapy or counselling, to address any underlying issues that may be contributing to your stress or burnout.

Another strategy for managing stress and burnout is to set achievable goals and to celebrate your successes along the way. It's easy to get caught up in the details and to lose sight of the bigger picture, so make sure to step back and take a bird's eye view of your progress. It's also important to be flexible and to adjust your goals as needed.

In summary, managing stress and burnout is an ongoing process that requires ongoing effort and attention. By recognizing the signs of burnout, setting boundaries and limits, practicing self-care, seeking support, and setting achievable goals, you can prevent burnout and maintain your motivation and productivity as a solo game developer.

If you find yourself struggling with stress or burnout, it's important to take action and seek help.

This can mean talking to a therapist or counsellor, seeking support from friends and family, or taking a break from game development to rest and recharge. Remember, your well-being is just as important as the success of your game and taking care of yourself is essential for long-term sustainability in the industry.

As a solo game developer, it's important to recognize the signs of stress and burnout and to take proactive steps to manage them. This can include prioritizing self-care, taking breaks when needed, and seeking help when necessary, such as through therapy or other forms of support.

While this chapter is meant to provide an overview of managing stress, it's important to note that it is by no means a comprehensive guide and that there are many other resources available for those struggling to cope with stress and burnout.

If you are feeling overwhelmed, both mentally and financially, it is crucial to seek professional help. **Don't be afraid to reach out for support and to take care of yourself.** Remember, your well-being is just as important as the success of your game development project.

Conclusion:

It's important to stay motivated and avoid burnout in order to be successful and sustainable in the long term. This can be a challenging task, especially when you are working on a project that is all-consuming and requires a great deal of time, energy, and effort. In this chapter, we discussed a range of strategies for setting goals and priorities, finding support and community, and managing stress and burnout. By following these tips and seeking help, when necessary, you can stay focused, energized, and engaged in your game development journey.

One of the most effective ways to stay motivated and avoid burnout is to set clear goals and priorities, and to create a roadmap for your game development journey. This can help you stay focused, avoid distractions, and make progress towards your objectives. It's also important to identify and prioritize the tasks and responsibilities that are most important to your game development, and to break down large tasks into smaller, more manageable steps.

Another key strategy for staying motivated and avoiding burnout is to find support and build a community of other game developers, mentors, or professionals who can provide guidance, encouragement, and a sense of camaraderie. Participating in online forums, communities, or events can be a great way to connect with like-minded individuals and learn from their experiences. Don't forget to also seek support from your friends and family outside of the game development industry, as they can provide a different perspective, emotional support, and a sense of balance in your life.

Managing stress and burnout is also crucial for maintaining your motivation and well-being. It's important to recognize the signs of stress and burnout, such as feelings of overwhelm, exhaustion, or frustration, and to take proactive steps to manage them. This can include prioritizing self-care, taking breaks when needed, and seeking help when necessary, such as through therapy or other forms of support.

It's also worth remembering that no one has all the answers, and everyone approaches game development differently. What works for one person may not work for another, so it's important to be open to trying new things and finding what works best for you. Don't be afraid to seek out advice and guidance from others and remember to take breaks and prioritize self-care.

Ultimately, the key to staying motivated and avoiding burnout is to find a balance between your game development pursuits and other areas of your life. By taking care of yourself and seeking support when needed, you can stay on track and achieve your game development goals.

In conclusion, staying motivated and avoiding burnout as a solo game developer requires a combination of setting goals and priorities, finding support and building a community, and managing stress and burnout. By taking the time to focus on these areas, you can stay motivated, sustain your business, and enjoy the rewards of your hard work and dedication to game development.

Chapter 7:
Recap of Key Points

Recap of key steps in solo game development process

As a solo game developer, you have a lot of responsibilities and tasks on your plate. The journey from idea to finished product can be a long and challenging one. It can be easy to feel overwhelmed or uncertain about how to proceed, especially if you are just starting out on your game development journey.

In this book, we've covered a wide range of topics that are important for solo game developers to consider. From the initial planning stages to marketing and distribution, the process of creating a game is complex and requires a wide range of skills and knowledge. These include:

- Idea generation and game design: Coming up with creative and innovative game ideas, and turning them into a detailed and cohesive game design. The first step in any game development project is to have a clear vision of what you want to create. This involves setting goals, identifying your target audience, and creating a roadmap for your project.

- Pre-production: Setting up a development plan, creating a prototype, and preparing for the actual development process. The design phase is where you start to bring your vision to life. This includes creating game mechanics, levels, characters, and other gameplay elements.
- Development: Building and testing your game, using various tools and techniques to bring your vision to life. The development phase is where you actually build your game. This involves programming, testing, and iterating on your design until you have a finished product.
- Marketing and distribution: Promoting your game and making it available to players on different platforms. Once your game is complete, it's time to start thinking about how you will get it into the hands of players. This involves creating a marketing plan, setting up a distribution platform, and promoting your game to potential players.
- Legal and financial considerations: Protecting your intellectual property, setting up a business or legal entity, creating contracts and agreements, and managing

budgets and finances. Legal and financial considerations are an important part of the game development process. This includes setting up a business structure, protecting your intellectual property, and managing your finances.

- Staying motivated and managing burnout: Setting goals and priorities, finding support and community, and managing stress and burnout. Solo game development can be a challenging and isolating process, and it's important to take care of yourself both mentally and physically. This includes setting goals, finding support and community, and taking breaks when needed.

Each of these steps is important in its own right, and they all contribute to the success of your game. By following the advice and guidance provided in this book, you can increase your chances of creating a great game and achieving your goals as a solo game developer.

It's important to remember that game development is a long and challenging process, and there will be times when you face obstacles and setbacks. However, by staying focused, staying motivated, and seeking support when needed, you can overcome these challenges and achieve your dreams.

So, take a moment to reflect on everything you've learned in this book, and think about how you can apply these concepts to your own game development journey. And don't forget to keep learning and growing as a game developer – there is always more to learn and discover in this exciting and dynamic industry.

Recap of challenges and strategies for overcoming them

As a solo game developer, you are likely to encounter a number of challenges and obstacles during the development process. These can range from technical issues to creative blocks, managing time, finding support and community, staying motivated and avoiding burnout, and navigating legal and financial considerations, and can be especially difficult to navigate when working on your own. However, it's important to remember that these challenges are a normal part of the game development process, and that there are strategies you can use to overcome them.

One key strategy for overcoming these challenges is to set goals and priorities, and to break down large tasks into smaller, more manageable steps. This can help to keep you on track and to make progress towards your goals. It can also be helpful to seek support from other game developers, mentors, or professionals, and to participate in online forums or communities. This can provide valuable guidance and a sense of camaraderie as you navigate the game development process.

Another strategy is to break down large tasks into smaller, more manageable steps. This can help you to stay focused and avoid getting overwhelmed by the amount of work that needs to be done. It can also be helpful to set clear goals and priorities, so that you know exactly what needs to be done and when.

And a third strategy for overcoming challenges is to seek support and guidance from others. This can come in the form of seeking advice from more experienced game developers, collaborating with others, or simply talking through your challenges with friends or family. By building a supportive network of people around you, you can feel less alone and more motivated to keep going.

Joining online forums or communities for game developers can be a great way to seek help and support from others in the industry. These communities often have a wealth of knowledge and experience, and members are often willing to share their insights and offer assistance to others. Participating in online forums or communities can also be a great way to network and make connections with other developers, which can be valuable for finding collaborators or seeking advice on specific topics. Additionally, many online communities have mentorship programs or offer opportunities for developers to connect with industry professionals. If you are struggling with a specific challenge or just need some guidance, don't be afraid to reach out to these communities for help.

Finally, it's important to remember to take care of yourself, take breaks when needed and to manage your stress levels. Self-care is a crucial part of maintaining your physical, emotional, and mental well-being, especially as a solo game developer where you may be constantly juggling a variety of tasks and responsibilities. By taking care of your mental and physical health, you'll be better equipped to tackle the challenges that come your way.

It's important to make time for activities that nourish your body and mind, such as exercise, meditation, or hobbies. It's also essential to listen to your body and take care of any physical or mental health concerns as soon as they arise. If you are feeling overwhelmed, it is important to seek help through therapy or other forms of support. Remember, there is no shame in seeking help and it is always better to address any mental or financial challenges as soon as possible.

In summary, the key steps in the solo game development process include identifying your game concept, prototyping and playtesting, creating a roadmap, managing your budget and finances, protecting your intellectual property, and staying motivated and avoiding burnout. By following these steps and using the strategies outlined above, you can set yourself up for success as a solo game developer.

Inspiration and Advice for Solo Game Developers:

Examples of successful solo game developers and their stories

As a solo game developer, it can be helpful to draw inspiration and guidance from the experiences and successes of others in the industry. There are many examples of successful solo game developers who have achieved great things on their own, and their stories can provide valuable insights and motivation.

One such example is Markus Persson, also known as "Notch," the creator of the hugely popular game Minecraft. Persson began developing Minecraft as a solo project in his free time, and it eventually grew into a massive success, selling over 200 million copies worldwide. Persson's story is a testament to the power of hard work, persistence, and vision, and serves as an inspiration for other solo game developers who are looking to make their mark in the industry. After years of hard work, Persson was able to turn Minecraft into a massive hit, selling over 200 million copies and earning him a place on Forbes' list of billionaires.

Another successful solo game developer is Anna Anthropy, the creator of games like Dys4ia and Triad. Anthropy is known for her unique and innovative approach to game design, which has earned her a devoted following and critical acclaim.

Other successful solo game developers include Andrew Spinks, the creator of Terraria, and Jonathan Blow, the creator of Braid. These developers, like Persson, started out as solo projects and eventually grew into major successes, proving that it is possible to achieve great things on your own in the game development industry.

Here are a few more examples of successful solo game developers and their stories:

- Rami Ismail is the co-founder of Vlambeer, a game development studio based in the Netherlands. He is known for his work on games such as Super Crate Box, Nuclear

Throne, and Ridiculous Fishing. Ismail has gained a reputation for his ability to create innovative, high-quality games on a small budget, and he often speaks about the importance of independence and self-sufficiency in game development.

- David S. Gallant is a solo developer based in Canada who is known for his controversial game, I Get This Call Every Day. The game, which simulates the experience of working in a customer service call center, sparked a heated debate about the nature of video games as art and the role of developers as social commentators. Gallant is an outspoken advocate for the rights of game developers and has used his platform to speak out about issues such as harassment and censorship in the industry.

- Terry Cavanagh is an Irish game developer who has gained fame for his quirky, challenging games such as Super Hexagon and VVVVVV. Cavanagh is known for his ability to create unique gameplay experiences that are both accessible and challenging, and he has won numerous awards for his work. In addition to his work as a solo developer, Cavanagh is also a co-founder of the Irish Games Association, which promotes the development of games in Ireland.

- Ryan Clark is the creator of Crypt of the NecroDancer, a popular indie game that combines elements of rhythm games with rogue-like dungeon crawling. Clark developed the game as a solo developer and has received widespread praise for its innovative gameplay and catchy soundtrack. He is known for his passion for game development and his willingness to take risks in pursuit of creating unique and memorable games.

Of course, it's important to recognize that the stories of these successful developers are just a few examples, and there are many other paths to success in game development. However, reading about the experiences and insights of these developers can be a valuable source of inspiration and guidance for solo game developers who are looking to make their mark in the industry. Whether you're just starting out or have been working in the industry for years, there is always room for growth and success as a solo game developer.

Tips and tricks for staying motivated and productive as a solo developer

As a solo game developer, it can be easy to get overwhelmed and lose motivation. Staying motivated and productive as a solo game developer can be a challenge, especially when you are working alone and don't have the support and accountability of a team. Here are a few tips and tricks that can help you stay on track and make the most of your time and energy:

- Set clear goals and priorities: Having a clear roadmap can help you stay focused and on track. Try using the SMART goal-setting method to set specific, measurable, achievable, relevant, and time-bound goals. It's important to have a clear sense of what you want to achieve and how you plan to get there. By setting specific, measurable, achievable, relevant, and time-bound (SMART) goals, you can stay focused and motivated as you work towards your objectives.

- Create a schedule and stick to it: Having a consistent schedule can help you stay organized and avoid feeling overwhelmed. Set aside dedicated blocks of time for work, breaks, and self-care, and try to stick to your schedule as closely as possible.

- Break tasks down into smaller chunks: Large, complex tasks can be intimidating and demotivating. Break them down into smaller, more manageable steps to make progress feel more achievable.

- Take breaks and prioritize self-care: Burnout is a real risk for solo game developers. Make sure to take breaks and prioritize self-care, whether that means getting enough sleep, exercising, or taking time to relax and recharge. Working long hours without breaks can lead to burnout and decreased productivity. Make sure to take breaks, both short and long, to rest and recharge. This can include activities like going for a walk, meditating, or engaging in a hobby.

- Find a supportive community: It's important to have a support system to help you stay motivated and on track. This could include friends, family, mentors, or other solo developers. Surrounding yourself with other game developers and supportive individuals can help you stay motivated and on track. Consider joining online forums or communities, or attending events and meetups, where you can share your progress, ask for advice, and get feedback.

- Stay organized: A cluttered workspace can lead to a cluttered mind. Invest in tools and systems that help you stay organized, such as project management software or a physical planner. Use tools and techniques like task lists, time tracking, and productivity apps to help you stay organized and focused on your work. Consider using the Pomodoro Technique, which involves breaking your work into focused 25-minute blocks, followed by short breaks.

- Celebrate your accomplishments: Don't forget to celebrate your successes along the way. Whether it's hitting a milestone, releasing a new update, or simply making progress on your game, it's important to take the time to appreciate your hard work.

- Seek help when needed: It's okay to ask for help or seek guidance from other developers, mentors, or professionals. Don't be afraid to reach out for support when you need it.

By following these tips and tricks, you can stay motivated and productive as you work on your solo game development project. Remember, it's a journey, and there will be ups and downs along the way. The important thing is to keep pushing forward and stay motivated to achieve your goals.

Final Thoughts and Next Steps

You are embarking on a journey that can be both rewarding and challenging. It's important to remember that you don't have to go it alone. There are many resources available to support you on your journey, including online communities, forums, and events. There are also a number of successful solo game developers who have gone before you and are willing to share their experiences and advice.

The process of creating a game from scratch is no small feat, and it takes a lot of hard work, dedication, and perseverance to see it through to completion. Whether you're just starting out or you're an experienced developer, there will always be challenges and setbacks along the way. However, with the knowledge and skills you've gained from this book, you now have the tools and resources to navigate these challenges and turn your game development dreams into a reality.

As you embark on your own solo game development journey, remember to stay motivated and stay true to your vision. It can be easy to get discouraged or to lose sight of your goals, but by setting clear goals and priorities, seeking support and guidance from others, and taking care of yourself, you can stay on track and stay motivated.

Another key to success is to never stop learning. The game development industry is constantly evolving, and there are always new tools, techniques, and technologies to explore. By staying up-to-date and continuing to learn and grow, you can stay ahead of the curve and continue to improve your skills and knowledge.

So don't be afraid to reach out and ask for help when you need it. Whether it's through online forums, professional organizations, or local communities, there are many resources available to help solo game developers succeed. So don't be afraid to reach out and connect with others in the industry. And don't be discouraged by setbacks or challenges. Every game developer, regardless of their experience or team size, faces challenges and setbacks. It's all a part of the process. The important thing is to stay motivated and keep moving forward.

As you continue on your journey, remember to take care of yourself and prioritize self-care. And don't forget to celebrate your accomplishments along the way. You are embarking on a rewarding and exciting journey as a solo game developer, and there is no telling what you will achieve. So embrace the challenges, stay focused on your goals, and enjoy the journey.

We hope that this book has been a valuable resource for you, and that it has given you the knowledge and confidence to embark on your own solo game development journey. Whether you're just starting out or you're an experienced developer, we wish you the best of luck and look forward to seeing the amazing games that you create!

Suggestions for further learning and resources

As you embark on your solo game development journey, it's important to continue learning and seeking out new resources to help you grow and improve as a developer. There are many different ways you can do this, such as through online courses, books, and events. Here are a few suggestions for further learning and resources that you may find helpful:

Online courses: There are many websites that offer online courses on various aspects of game development. Some popular options include Udemy, Coursera, and edX. These courses can be a great way to learn new skills or to brush up on ones you already have.

Books: There are countless books on game development that cover a wide range of topics. Some popular options include "The Art of Game Design" by Jesse Schell, "Game Engine Architecture" by Jason Gregory, and "The Game Maker's Apprentice" by Mark Overmars. These books can be a great way to dive deep into a specific topic or to get a broad overview of game development.

Events: There are many game development events held throughout the year, such as conferences, workshops, and meetups. Attending these events can be a great way to meet other developers, learn new things, and stay up to date on the latest trends and techniques. Some popular events include the Game Developers Conference (GDC), the Independent Games Festival (IGF), and the Boston Festival of Indie Games (BFIG).

It's also important to remember that you don't have to go it alone on your solo game development journey. There are many communities of developers and enthusiasts who are happy to share their experiences, offer advice, and provide support. Joining online forums or groups, such as the Game Developer's Association (GDA) or the International Game Developers Association (IGDA), can be a great way to connect with others and build a supportive network of peers.

By continuing to learn and grow as a game developer, you can continue to improve your skills and increase your chances of success. So, as you take your first steps as a solo game developer, remember to stay motivated, stay focused, and keep learning. With hard work, determination, and a bit of luck, you can turn your dream of creating games into a reality.

Closing thoughts and farewell

We hope that you have found the information and guidance provided here to be helpful and inspiring as you embark on your own journey as a solo game developer. As you embark on your solo game development journey, it's important to remember that there is no one "right" way to do things. Every developer has their own unique path, and it's up to you to find what works best for you. It's also important to remember that game development can be a challenging and stressful process, and it's okay to take breaks and seek support when needed.

As you move forward, be sure to continue learning and growing as a developer. There are many resources available online and in-person, such as game development conferences, online communities, and educational resources. Don't be afraid to reach out to other developers for advice or guidance, and don't be discouraged if you encounter setbacks or challenges along the way.

It's important to remember that game development is a constantly evolving field, and there is always more to learn and discover. Whether you're just starting out or have been working on your own games for a while, there are always new tools, techniques, and approaches to try out. It's important to stay open to new ideas and to continue learning and growing as a developer.

We hope that this book has provided you with valuable insights and information that will help you on your solo game development journey. As you continue to develop your skills and knowledge, we wish you the best of luck and encourage you to keep reaching for your dreams. Thank you for joining us on this journey, and we hope to see the amazing games you create in the future.

Good luck on your journey, and we wish you all the best as you create your own amazing games!